CH

Library of Congress Cataloging-in-Publication Data

Charlotte Girlz / Carma DeLane

ISBN 9780985489458

Front and Back Cover Design by The Intelligent Consulting Design Team and House of Ego Photography

www.intelligentpublishing.org

Charlotte Girlz

Carma DeLane

Table of Contents

Acknowledgments

House of Ego Photography
Smell the Smoke Media

Dedication

Special thanks to Anastasia Garcia and Stephan Midget who graced my cover. Thank you everyone who was involved with my vision for this book. Mother you continue to inspire me. Anything is possible with determination. I'm not just a rapper

Introduction

Meet the Girls

Clarke

"**W**ait! Baby stop! She'll be home soon," I whispered heavily, my fake moans exciting him.

"Fuck that bitch!" he moaned kissing my mouth harder and then my neck.

"Bastard!" I thought to myself, almost breaking my sexual trance.

I wanted to roll over, grab my nine millimeter, and pop his ungrateful cheating ass. His wife was a lawyer, a fucking breadwinner. She'd won cases all over the state of Ohio, so we knew this one would make headlines by morning. She held a late meeting to ensure that she had a believable alibi. Dawn was keeping close tabs on her to make sure she didn't change her mind, punk out, and try to call the police or something. I jumped on top lining my pussy up with his shaft.

"Oh, you wanna be a bad boy huh?" I asked seductively. He moaned in ecstasy as I pressed my wet clit against his dick in a grinding motion. I was disgusted. "You know what happens to bad boys don't you?" I leaned over and whispered in his ear being sure to secure my hard nipples against his chest. "They get punished!" I whispered.

His breathing became heavy with excitement. "Punish me baby!" he replied ignorant to my irony.

I hopped out of bed and headed towards the bathroom. He grabbed himself as he watched my perfect ass trot off. Standing in the mirror I almost puked inside my mouth. There was nothing attractive about this asshole. He was bald in the middle of his head, his chest was full of those nasty little curled up hairs, and he had a big fat stomach that made him look at least seven months pregnant. I mean c'mon, how couldn't he know something was up? He could never pull a woman like me. I turned the water on in his Jacuzzi tub and turned on the radio. Anger engulfed my body as I heard the song that was playing, Tina Turner's "*What's Love Got to Do With It*". I thought back to Clyde and all the hell he had put me through.

"Not a damn thing!" I whispered to myself.

"Baby!" he yelled out from the bedroom.

"What!" I yelled back aggravated, but quickly realized I needed to change my tone. "I'm coming!" I said pretending to be more interested and a lot more pleasant. I emerged from the bathroom flawless. My black slide in high heels matched my lingerie. My 36c's sat pretty in my Victoria Secret, and the see through underwear I was wearing made it easy to tell that my kitty had no fur. His dick was still at attention.

"What were you doing?"

"Running us some bath water. I wanna try something different," I said pulling his arms towards me.

"Oh, you wanna do it like that huh?"

"We can do it however you want daddy! Now come with me if you want to live," I signaled with my finger in a *come-hither* motion while chuckling on the inside.

He waddled his sloppy fat ass out of bed and into the bathroom, completely naive to what was about to take place.

"Get in!" I said forcefully and gave his rear end one hard slap. "Oh I like this!" he grinned eager to see what tricks I had up my sleeve.

I thought he'd overflow all the water, forcing me to resort to plan B, which could have gotten messy. I started to move to the music, swaying my hips and nibbling on my fingertips.

"Damn, that ass is fine!"

I picked up the radio and started to move toward the tub. He was so mesmerized by my ass he barely noticed.

"Really? How fine is this ass?" I questioned as I danced.

"Shit, I would pay for that ass!"

"Oh, you *will* pay for this ass," I said sarcastically still moving closer to the tub.

"How much you want for that ass? My wife can afford it. Now get that ass in this tub," he said reaching for me, but I dodged his grasp. "C'mon, you got a nigga catching blue balls."

I glared back at him for a few seconds with my ice-cold eyes.

"Just one more question."

"Anything!" he quickly responded.

I paused the music and there was only the sound of the dripping water faucet. I looked him dead in his eyes."Would you die for this ass?"

He eyeballed the radio and then me. Before he could answer, I dropped the radio in the tub. Sparks flew as his body jerked and splashed in the water. A few drops hit me in the face, but I didn't blink. The electricity in the bathroom went out. His skin sizzled and a disgusting smell filled the room. His body jerked one last time, before it went completely limp.

I returned to the bedroom, making sure to gather all of my things. I didn't bother to redress. I tied my trench coat around my figure eight frame. As my high heels clicked toward the door on his immaculate marble floor I flipped open my phone and dialed Charlotte. She picked up only saying one word.

"Yes?"

"It's done," I replied and we both hung up.

Every year more than one hundred and sixty men are reported missing in the city of Cleveland. Of those one hundred and sixty men, more than half of them are never found. Here's another fact for your ass! Every year about the same amount of men living in the city, admit to infidelity or cheating on their significant other. So does this mean that the women being cheated on are greatly responsible for a large percentage of this disappearance? Yes, but so are we!

I'm Clarke Williams. I've known Charlotte for as long as I can remember. We grew up together in the same foster home and have been inseparable ever since. See, me and Charlotte relationship is a little different than the rest of the girls. We hold a secret that we vowed to take to our fucking graves!

I used to be in a really abusive relationship. His name was Clyde Williams. He cheated on me, stalked me, you name it. I can't count how many times I went over to Charlottes house with a busted lip and a black eye. She always tried to get me to leave him, but I never listened. For eight years, I put up with his bullshit.

I'm a new woman now! I dare any nigga to even *look* like he wants to act up and I'll hand him his balls. Literally! Three miscarriages, two broken bones, two STD's, and I still couldn't find the strength to move on. It was the child pornography that finally made me snap. Our daughter was ten years old the last time I saw her. I couldn't stand to look her in her face and have to explain to her why mommy didn't help her all those years. So Danita lives with my mother now and I don't have contact with either of them.

I waited until I knew he was really into the tape so he could die with his dick in his hands! What? That bastard deserved it! In fact, if I could go back I wouldn't have let him off so easy. I would have made his ass suffer! It was like I was possessed. I emptied the clip, reloaded, and even when it was empty again, I kept squeezing the trigger. There was blood and brains all over the damn place and I was hysterical. The only person I could think to call was Charlotte. She raced over and helped me clean up the mess. We dumped the body in Lake Erie and swore we'd never tell a soul. The case is still unsolved so I guess you could say I owe Charlotte my life.

She's always been the smart one, so it surprised me when she brought the proposition to me. Killing for money was never on my agenda, but Charlotte said we did such a good job and it did feel good putting that fool out of his misery. We decided that we'd only assassinate men, but if a bitch got in the way she would get it too!

For a while, it was just Charlotte and me. We were so un-professional. I remember the first paid job we did. The asshole wouldn't die! He took seven bullets in his torso and was still squirming. That's why we're precise now. Aim for the head!

We watched a lot of criminal shows like; *CSI, Law and Order,* and *World's Dumbest Criminals,* the kind of shows that taught you how police caught the bad guys, which in turn taught us how *not* to get caught. I don't know how many men I've killed exactly, maybe a little over twenty. I try not to keep track. It's easier on your conscience that way.

Over time, we perfected our craft and decided we could be a hell of a lot more lucrative if we expanded, so we formed a team. Ten thousand dollars was the least we'd do a job for. We once did a job for a little over half a million; some senator guy. We use what we have, to get to who we want. Don't get it twisted. We're not some woman man haters club. Shit, I love dick! This is about the money, but I'd be lying if I said we didn't all share some common hate for men deep down, even Charlotte. Her dad beat her mom to death. That's how she ended up in foster care.

As for the other girls, there's Dawn, your typical biker rock chick, always in black, always in a belly top or something leather. Most people see her and assume she's mixed because of her milky complexion and hazel eyes, but she's just as black as the rest of us. Crazy, but black! Dawn is a straight up freak. She has six tattoos and five piercings, three of which can't be seen when she's fully dressed. She has no inhibitions. She's tried just about every drug on the market and had more sexual partners than all of us put together. I keep telling Charlotte her party girl ways are going to get us caught up. I knew Dawn had what it took when she handled Martin, some asshole who really got out of line at the club. She seduced him and convinced him into letting her tie him up. Then she took her panties off, soaked them in lighter fluid, stuffed them in his mouth, and lit a match! I had to give it to her. That was some bad shit! None of us really knows why Dawn assassinates. Her father was a doctor. When he was alive, he spoiled her rotten, so she isn't exactly hurting for cash. Quite honestly, I think the bitch is just sick and gets off on it!

Then there's Kenya. I know what you're thinking, typical hood chick right? Wrong! Kenya was running shit on her block, a dope girl if you will. Niggas answered to her and if you didn't have her money there would be hell to pay. Kenya's hate for men was fueled by her hate for her step dad. He molested her most of her childhood. He was our first job as a group, and that one was on the house. She took the long barrel of a forty four-caliber Rimfire pistol, shoved it up his ass, and pulled the trigger! I don't know what hurt worse, the bullet or the fact that she didn't use any lube. I think being molested really affected her because she's strictly pussy now. Kenya loves the look on a guy's face when he's sizing up her thick hips and caramel skin and she burst his bubble by telling him she's gay. Most guys don't buy it because she dresses feminine and isn't the type to grab her crotch. She can't stand butch lesbians who try so hard to impersonate men and just end up overdoing it. She has absolutely no attraction toward men, but she doesn't let her sexual preference get in the way of our business.

12

So there you have it. There's Charlotte the boss lady in charge, who gets the orders and collects the money. There's me, Clarke the mother figure and co-founder, Dawn the hard headed thrill seeking wild child, and Kenya the baby and hood chick. We call ourselves *Charlotte Girlz.* Women hire us to kill husbands, baby daddies, boyfriends, and exes. It may be for unfaithfulness. Hell it may even be for insurance money! Who gives a damn as long as we get our cut. This isn't any of that Charlie's Angel's bull shit! We are real trained assassins, whose identities must remain unknown. In fact, I only meet with Charlotte about once every three months and we all have jobs to remain discreet.

Dawn you guessed it, is a stripper. Kenya, left the block and now owns a clothing store, and I'm a legal secretary at a big law firm. I hate my job. Hell, I hate my boss. In fact, he may be our next hit. Huh, I'm kidding, lighten up. Bottom line, we are sexy sophisticated women and we have what all men want! *A night of passion with one of Charlotte Girlz could be your last!*

Chapter 1

A Woman Scorn

Kenya

It was almost eight o'clock, so Kenya was closing up the store. She cut the lights off and headed towards the alarm system.

"6-9-5-4," she whispered out loud.

"Area not secure," the alarm sounded.

"Stupid ass alarm! Waste of damn money," she yelled and banged on the keypad.

"6-9-5-4," she repeated rekeying the code.

"Area not secure," the alarm sounded again.

She turned and began to walk towards the light switch, but her movement was halted by a husky man's body in the darkness. Before she could reach for her Smith and Wesson his gloved hand was over her mouth and he was holding her so tight that her butt was pressed firmly against his crotch.

"Who's your connect?" he asked.

"Connect?" she replied muffled and puzzled.

"Bitch don't fuck with me. You can't tell me you left the drug game to sell fucking clothes!" he said giving her a jerk and tightening his grasp.

"Look I'm clean, I went straight!"

"Straight?" he laughed "Bitch ain't nothing straight about yo ass!

If I give you some of this dick, then you'd be straight," he said sarcastically, thrusting his pelvis into her ass.

She tried to free herself from his grasp, but he only squeezed harder.

"You know niggas in the hood is really upset that you done came up on a connect and you're not sharing. Especially after all that work we put in for you."

Kenya was trying her best to place his voice, but it was too muffled through the ski mask. "I'm watching you bitch!"

Before she could reply, a sharp pain pierced through her cheek and she felt blood trickling down her face. He ran towards the door his footsteps quickly getting distant. Kenya grabbed her gun and emptied the clip.

When she turned on the lights, he was gone. There were a few bullet holes in the window. She touched her face and glared at the blood on her fingertips hoping that she had at least grazed the bastard.

Dawn

Midnight was approaching and Dawn was on her way to Club Inter belt to set up a job. She pulled up in front and hopped off her all black Yamaha bike. Her windblown long jet-black hair fell perfectly into place. Her skintight jeans accented her apple bottom. She walked straight to the front of the line radiating confidence in her leather jacket and black knee high boots. The bouncer didn't hesitate to open the rope. Dawn turned around and gave him a wink, because she knew he'd be looking at her ass.

The club was full of strange characters; gays, straights, queers, and Drag queens. It was definitely Dawn's type of scene, but she wasn't here to party. Charlotte had assigned her to hit a man by the name of Norman Phillips. Norman was married to Janet Phillips. Janet's father had recently passed away leaving her a very large lump sum of money. Janet was set to inherit the riches on her thirty-second birthday, which was rapidly approaching. Norman was planning to have Janet killed and make out with the cash, but Janet had caught wind and planned to turn the tables. It was a two hundred and fifty thousand dollar job. Split four ways between all four girls that equaled out to be seventy five thousand a piece. Dawn had to bring her A game.

She sat down at the bar to have a drink. She reached in her back pocket and popped an ecstasy pill chasing it with a shot of Patron. That was nothing for her. She peered across the room and recognized Norman

16

from the picture Charlotte had supplied. He was a really clean cut nerdy looking guy. "*What the hell is he doing here?*" she thought to herself.

She knew Norman had already noticed her. Hell, she was the hottest chick in the club. When he made eye contact with her, she twirled a few strands of her hair around her index finger and licked her lips. He quickly looked down nervously. Dawn knew he wouldn't make the first move. She stood up and leaned over the bar exposing more than the smile of her back and signaling to the bar tender.

"What can I get you sexy?"

"Nothing!" she said teasing. "But, you see that guy over there in the suit?"

"You mean Steve Urkel?" he joked.

"Yeah, give him a cherry bomb on me!"

"I guess," the bartender responded. "Doesn't seem like your type, but it's your world sexy!" he said shrugging his shoulders.

A cherry bomb wasn't the manliest of drinks, but Dawn had a plan. When the bartender sat the drink in front of Norman, he pointed over at Dawn and she gave a little wave. Norman looked shocked, but lifted the drink as if to say *thank you* and took a sip. Dawn walked over and took a seat on the stool next to him. He looked increasingly uncomfortable as she closed the gap between them.

"You here alone?" she asked.

"Who me?" he said pointing to himself with clammy hands.

Dawn chuckled, "Who else silly?"

"Oh yeah, I'm alone. How about you?" he said looking around.

"Not anymore!" she said seductively.

His eyes widened as he took a gulp of his drink.

"How's the drink?"

"Oh, it's good. A bit strong, but good!"

"*Wimp*", she thought. "I love cherries," she said taking the cherry from his cup and licking it with the tip of her tongue before biting it off the stem. Norman shifted his weight in his seat several times and adjusted his tie.

"So what brings you to a club like this?"

"What do you mean?" he responded as if he didn't know he stuck out like a sore thumb.

"You just seem a little uptight for this. That's all," she smiled.

"No I'm down," he said in the nerdiest way possible.

"*Oh, really?*" she challenged.

"Yeah," he said sounding unsure of his own words.

18

"Drink up," she said emptying the remains of his drink into his mouth. "Well then dance with me!"

"No, I don't..."

Before he could complete his sentence, Dawn was on her feet removing his suit jacket and dragging him onto the dance floor. The lights and techno music seemed so intoxicating to Norman, but little did he know Dawn had slipped two crushed Date Rape pills into his drink while he was watching her make love to that cherry. She swung her hair and caressed herself as she danced around his stiff body. Other men looked on, their eyes green with envy and wishing they were in Norman's shoes. The music pulsated through his body and he seemed to loosen up a bit. Dawn was turned on too. She was the kind of girl who got off knowing she was wanted and it was obvious that Norman wanted her bad!

After about five songs of intense sexual chemistry, Dawn turned her body around, pressing her ass on his bulging pant zipper. She took him by the hand and pulled him into the bathroom. There were quite a few people standing around conversing, but she didn't care. She pushed Norman into a cramped stall and closed it behind them.

"What are you doing?"

"*What are you doing?*"she challenged.

She grabbed the back of his head and started to kiss him sloppily, her breath stained with alcohol and cigarettes. She could feel his manhood throbbing so she grabbed his ass with both hands and squeezed. She figured if he went both ways, then that would really get him hot. Norman let out a sigh. He did like it. Dawn knew she had to get him as open as possible if she was going to be able to lure him out of the club before the pills had reached their full potency.

People entered in and out of the bathroom, but that didn't seem to faze either of them. She unzipped his pants, spit in the palm of her hand, cupped his sack, and slid her hand from the base up to the head of his dick. Then she got down onto her knees and moved all of her long hair to one shoulder so he could have a clear view. She kissed and sucked his balls. Then she licked all the way up his dick in one smooth stroke with the tip of her tongue like it was a melting ice cream cone. She licked around the tip, completing one full circle. Norman let out a moan. Dawn kissed his mushroom head with her petite bubble gum pink lips and stood to her feet.

"Wait, please don't stop!" he begged.

Dawn handed him a small piece of paper with a phone number on it.

"What's this?" he asked.

"Call me if you wanna be spontaneous!" She looked him in his eyes. "You only live once right?" she said winking and then wiping her mouth.

"You mean sex...tonight?" he asked naively.

"What, you don't wanna fuck me? Could've fooled me!" she laughed.

"Yes, but I'm, I'm married!" he said feeling slightly guilty.

"Me too!" she lied. "It can be our little secret. We don't ever have to speak again after tonight," she reassured him.

"You mean like a one night stand?" he asked not ruling out the possibility.

"Call me. I won't wait forever," she said kissing him on the cheek.

He paused for a moment, weighing his options.

"But why me?

"Why not?" she answered cleverly.

She opened the stall door and left. Norman looked down at the paper still holding his dick in his palm. He could have jacked off, but she had peeked his curiosity. There was something about Dawn that was to die for.

It didn't take long for him to call. He was only sitting in his car about fifteen minutes before he folded. He didn't have to speak.

"There's a motel about a quarter mile down the road, get a room and leave the door unlocked."

The line clicked. He looked down at the phone verifying that she'd hung up. He was beginning to have second thoughts, but then he remembered how good she looked in those jeans sucking on that cherry. Thirty minutes later, his phone rang. He answered quickly, glad that she hadn't stood him up.

"Hello?" he tried to sound relaxed in the midst of all the anticipation. He was feeling a little groggy, but assumed it was due to what he considered to be an overindulgence of liquor.

"What room are you in?"

"Three O nine. Do you have a..."

She hung up again before he could finish.

"Condom," he said to himself finishing his sentence.

A few minutes later, the door creaked open. Norman was nervous, but still horny as hell.

"You know, I've never done this before."

Dawn pressed her index finger against his lips. "Don't talk. It's better that way!" She slid out of her jeans and tube top.

"You're not wearing any panties," he blurted out in shock.

Dawn's little B cups were perky enough to go braless. The site of her pierced clit and nipples instantly aroused him. She walked over to him wearing nothing, but her knee high boots and carrying a thin black sash.

22

"What's that for?" he asked.

"I'm going to blindfold you!" She walked behind him, threw her leg over his shoulder, and tied the sash.

"My wife is going to kill me if she finds out!" he whispered to himself.

"If you only knew," she whispered back.

"What's that?" Norman asked confused and jaded.

"I said I *really* want to fuck you!"

Dawn had to cover her mouth to keep from laughing. She walked over to her bag, pulled out her thirty-eight, and screwed on a silencer.

"What are you doing?"

"Look do you wanna do this or not? I can leave," she threatened.

"No, no please I'm sorry!" he said frantically.

Dawn walked over, stood directly in front of him, and took aim. He listened harder like a blind person who could sense someone close to them.

"Are you ready Mr. Phillips?" she asked.

"How do you... How... do you know... know my name?" he barely mumbled.

"Your wife told me!"

23

Before he could take off the blindfold, a single bullet sunk into the middle of his forehead killing him instantly upon impact. Overall, he wasn't too bad of a guy. He just wanted a good fuck. So she decided to make it less painful. She reached in his pocket and took the little piece of paper with her prepaid phone number on it. After dressing, she hopped on her bike and called Charlotte.

"Yes?" Charlotte said.

"Handled that," Dawn answered and sped off into the night.

Clarke

It had been a while since we'd hit a job that required all three of us to finish. If it was a job that required two girls Charlotte usually sent Dawn and Kenya. I rolled solo most the time.

"Everything's in place," Dawn confirmed into the phone.

"Keep your eyes on her," I responded referring to the girlfriend of a twenty seven year old dope boy, I was assigned to take out.

I didn't make a habit of hanging out in the projects, but it was an in and out job. The reason for the hit was never disclosed, but we figured the money was probably dirty considering the line of work he was in. Monique was his typical ghetto baby mama, but she was obviously a little smarter than she let off. The plan was to catch Andre on the elevator near their fifth floor apartment. Then take it to the basement, which was vacant, and exit through the urine stained stairwell, where Kenya would be waiting to pull off.

Normally our hits required a little more finesse and discretion, but in this neighborhood, the sound of a bullet was like a doorbell. Dawn was downstairs in a parking lot across the street from the apartment's playground keeping an eye on Monique who was pushing her two year old in a swing and looking at least ten months pregnant.

Andre had a lot of enemies. Not to mention the amount of strung out crack heads who would split his wig for a hit of magic dust, so the cover up would be easy. Every day before he left to make his sells he would yell out the window to Monique downstairs.

"Monique, get yo ass in the house! It's gettin dark. Whatchu think this is Beverly Hills or some shit! Don't make me come and get yo nappy head ass girl!"

Monique rolled her eyes and continued pushing her daughter on the swing. I was holding the elevator at the basement level when I got the call from Dawn. I answered.

"He's moving out!" she said quickly and hung up the phone.

The rise of the elevator seemed so slow as it crept toward the fifth floor. The bell chimed and echoed in my ears. The sturdy doors opened to reveal a decent looking young man dressed in an outfit that seemed out of his budget. I knew he had a gun, so my shot had to be accurate and effective. Andre's lustful eyes quickly sized me up in my interpretation of an "around the way" girl outfit. My heavy hoop earrings hung next to my excess baby hair, my lips covered in gloss.

"Can I ride with you?" he asked smirking and with no remorse for his pregnant girlfriend who was just downstairs.

I popped my gum, blew a seductive bubble, and leaned back on the elevator walls crossing my arms.

"Boy just push the damn button!"

"Be like that then bitch!"

Rage took over every limb of my body. I felt tingling in the tips of my toes and my ears began to warm. There was something about that word. I didn't tolerate any man calling me the B word! I lost my cool. As Andre reached to push the button, I delivered one nearly point blank shot to the back of his head. Even though gunshots were normal in this part of town, the chilling sound filled Monique's heart with regret, forcing her to scoop up her daughter and run towards the building. She panted as she tired easily hoping it wasn't too late.

Blood splatter covered the elevator walls. Andre slumped to his knees and fell over blocking the elevator door from closing. I felt my cell phone vibrating in my pocket, but I was in no position to answer it.

Down on the first floor Monique frantically pushed the up button, becoming increasingly frustrated when she realized the elevator wasn't moving. I struggled to pull the dead weight of Andre's upper body back onto the elevator. Monique turned towards the steps, but quickly realized her pregnant body could never overcome five flights of stairs with a two year old on her hip.

I needed to make a decision fast. I poked my head out of the elevator, looked both ways, and spotted a door at the end of the hallway that read stairwell. I put on my sunglasses and booked it towards the door. As fast as I was running I couldn't stop fast enough and collided with a woman climbing the stairs, knocking her flat on her ass. When I looked at her, she appeared stunned. Silence surrounded us. She put her hand over her mouth as if she wanted to scream, but no sound would come out. She widened her eyes as she glared at the blood on my shirt. Tears welled up in her eyes and that's when I realized who she was. It was Monique. I was reaching for my gun when I heard the pitter patter of little feet.

"Mommy!" her daughter screamed with excitement as she tried to wrap her arms around her mother's waist.

I looked at the little girl, at Monique's belly, and finally I stared Monique back in the eyes. She had seen my face long enough to point me out in any line up. I knew what I had to do next would probably haunt me for the rest of my life, but there was no way around it. I yanked the little girl away from her.

"Please, don't! I won't say anything. Don't take my baby!" she begged.

I covered the eyes of the little girl, without hesitation, I shot and killed Monique. The little girl screamed and cried her vision blinded by my hand. The sound of the loud gunshot frightened her. When I made it out Kenya had her foot on the gas ready to make a clean get away. I quickly sat the little girl in the grass and jumped in the passenger seat.

"What's up with the kid?" Kenya questioned.

"Drive!" I demanded and she hit the gas.

Chapter 2

Man Eater

Sunshine beamed through the bare windows of Dawn's downtown loft, waking her from her sleep. Squinting her eyes, she looked over at the alarm clock while wiping the drool from her mouth. She'd been asleep since the hit with me and Kenya yesterday evening. It was 11:07am.

"Fuck!" she exclaimed jumping out of bed and running towards the bathroom.

Dawn liked to work the club early because she didn't have to deal with young ass wanna be hustlers who thought that just because they had a stack of singles covered with a few twenties, that they deserved a private dance. Dancing in the daytime meant a lot of corporate white men sneaking off on their lunch breaks, just looking to get a quick peek at a black pussy.

Dawn quickly brushed her teeth and followed up with two swigs of Jack Daniels, which was on her bathroom sink. She didn't use a chaser. She splashed water through her long black hair, so that it would curl at the ends, and then pulled it into a tight ponytail straight to the back. She didn't even bother to freshen up. She just splashed on some Diesel perfume and hopped in her car.

When she arrived at the club, some new girl was sliding down the pole to Nelly Furtado's "*Man Eater*". Dawn didn't pay her much attention. There were always new girls at the club. She saw Paul, one of her regulars and blew him a kiss. Paul always came on Fridays to get a private dance from Dawn. Occasionally she'd throw in a blow job, not because she needed the extra money, but because she just liked giving head.

She went in the back and opened up her locker. She pulled out a small vile filled with cocaine. She poured some onto her car key and quickly sniffed it up. She grabbed a black thong from her bag and slipped it on with her stripper shoes. Most of the girls liked to dress up in cute little outfits, but not Dawn. She figured, *shit you're gonna get naked anyway.* Guys just wanna see it. They don't wanna have to sit through a movie! That was her philosophy. She didn't even opt to put on a top.

When she emerged from the locker room, she saw the new girl taking Paul into the back for a private dance. She knew she'd have to lay down some ground rules for the bitch later.

When it's your turn to dance, you tell the D.J. three songs you want him to play. For the first song, you just dance. For the second, you take off your top and the third, your bottoms. Dawn always danced to just one song. She didn't need three songs to make as much money as the other girls and they hated her for that. It was something about her grungy *don't give a fuck* attitude that made her irresistible to customers.

Plies, "*Ms Pretty Pussy*" was the song of her choice. Dawn danced around the pole, clapping her ass and squeezing her pussy muscles in the faces of the paying customers. She slid down the pole a few times and hung upside down without using any hands, as the men looked on in amazement. Three hundred dollars easy and there were only about eight guys in the club, not to mention what she was about to make from private dance requests.

When she finished she walked over to the bar and the bar tender had a shot of Patron sitting on the counter for her. She threw it back.

"Thanks Dave!" she yelled over the music.

Dawn looked around the room for Paul, her regular, but he was nowhere in sight.

"Damn, that bitch must really be putting in some work!" she thought.

She headed towards the back, pushing aside beaded curtains and peering into each V.I.P. room looking for Paul. She called out for him.

"Paul I know you're not cheating on me!"

She reached the last door of the hallway, which was closed. She put her ear to it, to see if she could hear any sounds of money being made. She tried to open the door, but something seemed to be blocking it.

"Paul?" she called confused. There was no response. "Oh, I know this bitch ain't stealing *my* paying customers?" she whispered getting aggravated.

Dawn pushed with all of her might. The door flew open and a chair hit the floor. Across the room, Paul sat with his back facing Dawn. His pants were around his ankles and the new girl was kneeling in front of him.

"I see we're gonna have to lay down some rules for her Paul!" she said waving index finger in the air. Paul still didn't answer. The closer Dawn walked the more uncomfortable the girl seemed to get. "Was is that good Paul? You're speechless?" Dawn teased throwing her hand on his shoulder.

She jumped back when she realized Paul's head was slumped and the bitch had a wad of cash in her hands. Dawn peered at the girl shocked, but deeply impressed. She turned and began walking towards the door. In fear that she was going for help, the girl called out. "Wait! He's not dead, I only drugged him."

Dawn closed the door with no intensions of telling anyone anything.

"It's my own recipe, mostly Morphine. When he wakes up he won't remember anything!"

"How do I know that?" Dawn lifted one eyebrow challenging the girl.

She frantically stuffed half the money into Dawn's hands. "I'm Ebony," she said extending her hand.

Dawn slapped Ebony's hand out of her path. "Don't fuck with anymore of my regulars! You got it?" she said as serious as a heart attack.

"Yeah, I got it," Ebony said with a slight attitude that implied she wanted to beat Dawn's ass, but couldn't due to the circumstances.

Dawn snatched the other half of the money from Ebony's grasp, stuffed it in her panties, and shut the door behind her.

"Hell nah!" she thought to herself shaking her head as she headed back to the floor.

Clarke

Three shots left the barrel of my nine millimeter, and found their target piercing through the head of the paper mannequin.

"Beautiful shot!" a voice said from behind me.

I lifted my protective glasses and turned around to meet face to face with a handsome man in his early thirties smiling at me. His face was blemish free. He was a good five to six inches taller than I was. His arms were and shoulders were nicely chiseled, but not over done. His hands were clean, but strong and his sideburns were methodically connected to his shaped up beard. He was a Boris Kodjoe type, only darker with deep brush waves. Sexy!

"Thanks," I said dryly trying to keep it short.

"I've never seen you here before and I'm pretty regular," he said. "So."

There was a moment of silence. "So are you new?" he asked pleasantly.

"Do you always engage in conversation with people who don't seem to be giving you the time of day?" I snapped back trying to bruise his ego.

"No, but you seem worth the embarrassment!"

I paused for a second not knowing how to respond. It had been a while since a man had flattered me; not to mention he was fine as hell. He compensated for my hesitation. "So what's a pretty lady like you doing in a place like this, and with a gun like that?"

"I live in a rough neighborhood," I lied.

"Oh really? Sounds like you need a man, not a gun!" he teased.

"King is all the man I need!" I said kissing my gun. "He's faithful, protective, and very low maintenance."

"So what are the chances I could take you out to dinner *without* King?" he flirted charmingly as the dimple in his right cheek sank deeper.

"I don't do dinner! I said firmly trying to talk over the loud shots echoing in the background.

"Does that mean you don't do dinner or just don't want to do dinner with me?" he smiled exposing his perfect white teeth.

"I don't do dinner," I said even more firm.

"So what do you like to eat?" he said ignoring my attitude. "Men!"

I turned and looked him dead in the eyes to intimidate him. I couldn't stand a coward. He only chuckled.

"Cute, very cute. I'm Gregg, Gregg Thomas," he said reaching out to shake my hand.

This threw me off. Acting like a bitch was usually effective for me when chasing off a man.

"Clarke."

"Clarke?" he said suggestively asking for my last name. I quickly made one up. I'd already fucked up by giving him my real first name.

"Jones," I lied. "*How common!*" I thought to myself on the inside as I struggled to hide my blushing on the outside. He really had me open.

"Well it was nice to meet you Ms. Jones. Hopefully I'll see you   around again. Maybe you'll change your mind about dinner."

He walked away and I let out sigh of relief. I hadn't been that nervous since I'd met my deceased husband Clyde.

"Hey Clarke!"

I turned around and rolled my eyes, as if to say *what now nigga?*

"What's your favorite restaurant? Maybe I'll bring dinner to you." "Not KFC," I said sarcastically under my breath and thinking how tacky. Though I did love some chicken, any man who would take his girl to a fast food joint had no class.

"I'll surprise you." He said turning the corner.

Damn, he was fine. I had to give him that, but not fine enough to pass up filet mignon for a piece of dry ass chicken! Besides, my body looked better than it did at eighteen and that was due to a strict diet and five hundred sit-ups a day. A shot from the next lane woke me from my daze. It was 5:30. I needed get going if I was going to meet with Charlotte tonight.

Kenya

The logs in the fireplace burned slowly as Rick and Kenya listened to Jazz. Kenya hated Jazz. She was more of a hip-hop kind of girl, but she had to play the part. Kenya had been dating Rick for about a month and a half. At least that's what he thought. Charlotte had assigned her to hit Rick about two months ago. Rick wasn't the kind of guy you could pick up at a bar or a club. She had to put in a little work to catch him. Rick owned his own construction company and was the type of man most sensible women desired. He was a provider, took care of his kids, and wasn't bad looking. He was in the middle of an ugly custody battle with his soon to be ex-wife. She wasn't exactly the picture perfect mom and really didn't deserve those kids. Her issues with drug use and unemployment didn't exactly paint a motherly picture for the judge. Having Rick killed was the only way she could think of to win the case. No judge in the world was going to give her those boys, so unfortunately with Rick out of the picture they'd probably end up in the system.

Rick had driven Kenya to the mountains to spend the weekend at his log cabin he'd built a few years back. His wife never wanted to go. Kenya knew he planned to introduce her to his boys soon so she needed to cut it short and fast. Not to mention Tawnya, Kenya's girlfriend was getting a little suspicious of Kenya being missing in action all the time.

Rick held Kenya close in his arms. "I think I'm falling for you girl."

He kissed her on the forehead and then on her lips. This was the part she hated. Kenya kissed him back, wishing it could all be over and done with.

"What's wrong *Keisha* you seem distant?" he asked Kenya.

"I'm fine. I just have to use the bathroom."

"I'll be waiting," he said administering a slap to her ass.

Rick was so sweet, but in the bedroom, he was hard and rough. He liked to be dominant. Long and deep was his only technique. He was the kind of man that would grab you by the neck or push your face into the pillow while he fucked you from behind, ignoring your cries to ease up. Kenya hated that. The forcefulness reminded her so much of her stepdad molesting her when she and Rick had sex.

In the bathroom, Kenya took a deep breath. She'd never had to kill someone who she knew truly didn't deserve it. She drenched her fingers in KY jelly and stuck them up her pussy, hoping it wouldn't have to go that far. She pulled her magnum out of her overnight bag and loaded it then shoved it under the bed in the room. Rick startled her when she rose to her feet.

"Whatcha doing? Don't run from this dick!" he said thinking his dirty talk excited her.

He lifted her clear off the floor and sat her on the edge of the bed. He raised his shirt and tucked it under his chin so he could unbutton his pants. When he pulled his dick out it was already rock hard. Kenya's stomach got weak. He jammed his tongue down her throat and gripped her long french braids tightly. Kenya was furious, but not in reach of her gun.

"You know you like it rough baby!" he said pushing her head towards his dick.

She had no choice, but to suck it. He reared his head back in pleasure as Kenya's wet warm mouth sucked up and down. He pushed the back of her head forcing his dick deep in her throat. Kenya began to gag and almost threw up.

"Yeah, swallow this big dick!"

Rick was like another person. Kenya's eyes began to water as he moved her head faster, pushing his dick deeper and deeper into her mouth. He forced her onto her knees on the floor. She felt helpless, still unable to reach her gun. She started to have flashbacks of how her stepfather would touch her and a surge of anger fell over her body. In a rage, she bit down as hard as she could on Rick's manhood.

"Fuck! Bitch!" he screamed out slapping her to the floor out of pure reflex. "Keisha, what the fuck is wrong with you?" he yelled clenching his dick.

"My name ain't Keisha, its Kenya!" she said peering back at him. "Hoe, have you gone mad?" he fired still massaging himself with an expression of disbelief.

Kenya's magnum was starring her in the face. She grabbed it and pointed at him.

"Whoa! Bitch...I mean, we can work this out! I thought you were into that. Keisha, please baby I got kids!" he pleaded.

Kenya fired five shots into his chest. Ricks' body fell back on the bed.

"I said my name ain't Keisha!" She dropped the gun and it made a loud thud on the floor. Tears began to pour down her cheeks. She looked at his lifeless corpse and had to sprint to the bathroom to relieve her vomit in the toilet. She lifted her head up to the mirror and got sicker after seeing a picture of Rick's boys taped to it. She buried her face deep in the toilet bowl as she gagged and cried her eyes out. She sat there on the bathroom floor trying to gather herself knowing that she had fucked up and if Charlotte found out then she would have a bullet in her head too.

As one of *Charlotte Girlz,* she had a strict set of rules to live by and she had violated most of them tonight.

1. Loyalty. If you get caught you go down alone.

2. Never tell a hit your real name or any other personal information.

3. Always use a condom. (We didn't need any dead baby daddies, or DNA lying around.)

4. Never catch feelings.

5. Never speak about jobs over the phone or engage in conversation with Charlotte.

6. Finish the job within a three-month period.

7. Never make overly expensive purchases.

8. Attend self-defense, and shooting classes.

Lastly, no boyfriends. It would just make things complicated.

Kenya cleaned up and headed back to town. She never called Charlotte.

Clarke

I caught the East train to the city's limit, then a taxi the rest of the way, and Charlotte driver got me from there. I was so excited to see her. It had been months. Charlotte was the definition of a boss bitch. I'd never seen her not on her shit. Her ten thousand plus square foot house made it obvious that she was taking a little off the top before dishing the money out to us. I couldn't knock it though she *was* supplying the jobs. Charlotte had always been secretive about the way she found our jobs. Even I had no clue. "Some things are better left unsaid." She once said and never mentioned it again. I suppose if she revealed her method to us, we'd have no use for her.

I rang the buzzer twice and then once long. The door clicked and I made my way upstairs to the office where we always met. Charlotte's house was bad. A winding staircase and vaulted ceilings drew your attention to her extravagant chandelier hanging in the center of the room. She had class and her taste was definitely upscale. I opened the two wide doors to her office, which was dimly lit. Dead ahead was her desk. Her chair was facing the window as she looked out at the sparkling city lights in the distance.

"Charlotte?"

Her chair spun around slowly. She let out a puff of smoke just before putting out her cigar.

"You're late!" she said seriously.

"Bitch please! Save that Scarface shit for Dawn and Kenya!"

We both exploded with laughter. She stood up and met me for a hug.

"You look good," I said stepping back to look at her outfit.

She was wearing a tapered to fit, white Chanel suit with matching scarf. It complimented her thick coke bottle shape.

"Always," she bragged confidently with a smile. "So do you."

I plopped down in a chair across from her and she sat back down behind the desk.

"Watch it! Those are Italian," she blurted out. Charlotte had always been a little uptight. Okay, she was a no nonsense kind of girl, but I guess that made her a good businesswoman.

"So how much we talking?" I asked.

"Well business is kind of slow, just three this time," she replied.
"Three? Three isn't gonna keep me looking this pretty!" I joked.

Charlotte looked at my Prada bag and matching sunglasses. "Oh, I think you'll make due."

I rolled my eyes and poured myself a glass of Cristal champagne she had sitting in an ice bucket on her desk. I drunk it down and slammed the glass.

"So run em' down to me!"

She lifted my glass and placed a coaster underneath it. "Alright, asshole number one is Quincy Morgan. Apparently, he likes picking up prostitutes. Only problem is he's been married for thirty five years. This one's pretty straight forward. He's in his seventies, but it's one hundred and fifty thousand. I think he'd be more Dawn's speed", she smiled.

"Yeah I think so too," I cosigned in disgust. "Speaking of Dawn, that girl…"

"*That girl* is an asset to this team!" she cut me off. "I mean I can let her go, if you're willing to handle jobs like Mr. Morgan," she teased.

"Next!" I said escaping her sarcasm.

"Michael Hornsby. His mom just passed. He's the beneficiary."

"See, it's the greedy bitches like that I don't understand. I'm sure his wife is gonna see some of that money!" I snapped.

"Actually his aunt hired us," Charlotte said nonchalantly.

"His aunt?" I exclaimed.

"Look, it's not our job to decide who's right and who's wrong. It's our job to finish the job!" she said bringing me back down to earth.

I poured another class of champagne.

"And last, but not least Gregg Thomas. You may have seen him before. He shoots at your range. He's in his early thirties, typical pretty boy. He's cute. If I was still in the field I'd do him myself!" Charlotte laughed.

I damn near choked on my Champagne. "Who?" I said clearing my throat.

"Gregg Thomas. I take it you've seen him?" she asked handing me a napkin.

"No!" I quickly answered. "Went down the wrong pipe," I lied.

My mind flashed back to the shooting range and the dinner invitation Gregg had given me just hours before. "So what's his story?" I was anxious to know. I knew he was too good to be true.

"Nothing too much. It's an ex-girlfriend, one of those can't live with you; won't live without out you kind of broads. She wanted him back and he refused. I guess she figures if she can't have him, nobody will! The bitch seemed a little looney to me!"

I drifted back to Gregg's gorgeous smile.

"Always the good ones," I thought.

"Hello?" Charlotte interrupted my daydream. "'Are you okay? You seem a little unfocused."

"I'm fine," I said convincingly.

"Well I think you should handle this one."

"Me?" I said pointing to myself.

"Yes you! You're probably his type. He's into the relationship thing. Dawn's a little too out there and Kenya, well I think you'll enjoy this one a little more than Kenya. You'll probably have to play girlfriend for a while, but he shouldn't be a problem."

I sat in a daze.

"Are you sure you're okay?" she asked sounding more concerned.

"Yeah, I'm good."

"So what's going on with Kenya?"

"What do you mean?" I responded clueless.

"She didn't call me."

"She didn't? I'm having dinner with them tomorrow. I'll find out," I assured her.

"Please do. That's not like her," she added.

"Girl please, Tawnya probably has her somewhere laid up munching carpet!" I joked bringing back the relaxed mood.

We laughed simultaneously. The rest of the night consisted of; Moscato, catching up, and reminiscing on old times and how mischievous we were as teens.

Chapter 3

Devil in a blue Dress

It was about seven o' clock when I pulled up to *Donna's Lighthouse,* a sea food restaurant on the Westside. It was an upper class place, so I wore appropriate attire. I saw Dawn's and Kenya's cars which meant they'd probably already gotten a table. We always chose a different restaurant to meet at. The hostess greeted me wearing a clean white collar shirt and impeccably creased pants.

"Reservation, or would you like a table for one?" she asked.

I looked over her shoulders to see if I could spot the girls.

"Maam?" she raised an eyebrow.

"I have a reservation for *Lorena Lopez.*"

Everyone knows who Lorena Bobbit is and Lisa "Left Eye" Lopez was the rap chick who burned down her boyfriend's million-dollar mansion. We'd come up with that name to avoid using our own and figured why not have a little fun with it.

"Right this way Ms. Lopez,"

I smiled and followed. Kenya and Dawn sat at a table nestled in the back of the restaurant, in a section for high paying customers. It was illuminated by chandeliers and came with a complementary bottle of wine.

It was just my style. I removed my coat and the hostess asked if I wanted to check it.

"No I'm fine, but I will start with water, no ice, and extra lemon. Please not from the tap. Fiji if you have it, if not Dasani will just have to do."

She just stood there as if she was waiting for more instructions. "That'll be all."

I got comfortable in my chair and realized that Dawn and Kenya were staring at me. "What?" I questioned.

"See that's why we don't like to go nowhere with yo stuck up ass!" Kenya laughed.

"Okay, knowing she from Longwood Projects, born and raised," Dawn chimed in.

"Anywhere, don't like to go *anywhere*!" I corrected her.

They looked at each other and laughed in unison.

"Well, we should have went *anywhere* but, here and I do mean anywhere! Do you see these prices? I could've gone for some Mickey D's," Kenya rolled her eyes.

I shook my head. "We're here to discuss business and business isn't going so good right now. We only have three jobs, but Charlotte promises more," I reassured them.

"You will never believe what happened to me at work the other day," Dawn interrupted.

"Can it wait?" I said trying to keep things professional.

"No, this can't wait. This is some urgent shit!"

"Let me guess. You balanced three dicks on your head all at one time?" Kenya teased.

"No, but sucking dick is good for your skin. You should try it. That's why you're always so tense. You need some dick!" Dawn fired back.

I threw my hands up. I felt like a mother trying to break up a spat between her two daughters.

"Get to the point Dawn!" I urged.

"Hoe!" Kenya provoked Dawn.

"Dike!" Dawn returned the favor.

"You know what? I didn't come here for this!" I said sternly grabbing my coat off the chair beside me.

They both laughed as though *I* was the joke.

"No, *she* needs some dick!" Kenya laughed harder.

"Yeah, I'll give you that one," Dawn slapped Kenya a high five.

I twisted my lips up and crossed my arms.

"Okay, okay, so I was at work right? I had just finished dancing. I go to the back to find one of my regular customers, and this new bitch has him in a V.I.P. room, drawers around his ankles!"

"So! Isn't that what you strippers do?" Kenya said sarcastically taking a sip of her wine.

Dawn went on, ignoring her smart remark. "So I go to check the both of them, and he ain't moving. To top it off this bitch has a hand full of cash. She slipped him a mickey! Then she offers me half the money not to snitch!"

"So you took it right? Kenya asked.

"What do think? Hell yeah, I took it!"

"So what's your point Dawn?" I asked even more aggravated.

"I'm just saying, maybe you and Charlotte should look into it. She could be a potential member, that's all!" she said shrugging her shoulders.

"Yeah, that's just what we need, another stripper!" Kenya laughed.

"Just because she robbed some desperate corporate white guy, doesn't mean she could do what we do, but I'll have Charlotte look into it. Can we get back to business now?" I interjected. "Dawn, your guy is a little older. He's into the strawberry scene. Charlotte   recommended you."

"Older? Dawn turned up her lip. "How old is older?

"He's in his mid seventies!" I replied nonchalantly.

50

"Seventy? That's old enough to be my damn grandpa's grandfather. Me and the boss lady are gonna have to have a talk about these dummy missions she keeps sending me on. I'm gonna need raise or something! How much does it pay?"

"A hundred and fifty thousand," I said without looking up from my menu, knowing she'd have a change of heart.

"Shit, for a hundred and fifty G's I'll give his old ass a heart attack! I won't even have to use my gun," she said thrusting her hips in her seat. "Shit, for a hundred and fifty thousand Kenya will fuck his old ass! Right Kenya?"

I gave her a look a mother gives her child when they're doing something they know they have no business doing. She quickly took a sip of her water while Kenya giggled.

"What the hell are you laughing at? Charlotte said you never called her and what the fuck happened to your face?

"My cell was dead and..."

The waitress interrupted placing down their plates. "Lobster and filet mignon."

"Smells good. Thank you," Dawn tried dismissing her.

"Oh, you bitches ordered without me?" I said reaching across the table with my fork and stealing some of Dawn's   steak.

51

"I'll have the same, medium rare," I added catching her before she left.

"No problem," she said pouring my bottled water into a wine glass.

"Oh, I see all that manners and proper English shit just went out the window huh?" Dawn said cutting into what was left of her steak. "You still haven't answered my question Kenya. What happened to your face?" I quickly turned the mood serious.

"Man that bitch Tawnya! You know how these hoes are. They think you're cheating and they wanna act a fool," she lied pulling her long French braids onto her shoulder. "We got into a little scuffle."

"A little scuffle?" Dawn questioned. "It looks to me like she beat yo ass!" she laughed."Keep your phone charged! Your guy is Michael Hornsby," I said sliding her a folder. "Read it and burn it."

"Well, if he looks anything like baby boy at two o' clock, that shouldn't be a problem. He is sexy, but his girl is busted! Cute dress though," Dawn said looking over her Christian Dior glasses and taking a bite of her steak.

"Blue really isn't my color, but I would do him!" Kenya agreed.

"Girl bye!" Dawn shrugged her comment off.

I hesitated a few seconds before turning around to check him out. I almost fell out of my chair when I turned and saw Gregg, and with a woman at that. I tried to turn back around before he saw me, but I guess I starred a little too long because we made eye contact. I cleared my throat.

"Unbelievable," I spat.

"Told ya!" Dawn said.

"*Lying Bastard!*" I thought to myself.

I don't know why I was so upset with Gregg. Hell, he wasn't my man. Besides, many of men had tried deceiving me in the past. Why would he be any different?

The waitress sat my plate in front of me. It looked marvelous, but I had no intension of staying.

"Excuse me? Can I have a to-go box?" I tapped her.

It was really tacky to ask for one of those in such an upscale restaurant, but I didn't have much of a choice. "Sure, give me just a minute," she said, looking annoyed by all of my special request, but happy my ass was leaving. I could tell she was getting really aggravated with me.

"I'm going to the bathroom. Can one of you hook that up for me?"

They both looked at me confused.

"So you can ask the waitress for everything, but a doggy bag!" Dawn joked.

They laughed and drifted off into girl talk as though their argument had never even happened. I slipped off.

I waited in the bathroom for a few minutes and checked out my reflection. Just in case Gregg and crossed paths, I wanted him to see what he was missing out on. I looked good tonight! A hell of a lot better than his simple ass date. I peeked out of the bathroom and when I didn't see them waiting to be seated I figured the coast was clear.

"Clarke!"

I looked up to see Gregg and his date sitting at the table with Kenya and Dawn. "*Shit*!" I thought and felt my facial expression saying the exact same thing, so I put on a fake semi-smile. "Hello Gregg," I said taking a seat at the table.

"I thought you didn't do dinner?" He interrupted me before I could answer. "So, I was just telling Beatrice and Keisha how you've got the best shot at the range."

"*Beatrice*?" I thought as I smiled at Dawn for choosing   such   a stupid name. "Aren't you going to introduce me to your   lovely   date?" I said knowing I wasn't serious. The girl was hit.

"Oh, I'm so sorry. This is my little sister Jazmine. She's in town and I'm taking her out to celebrate. She's graduating from college."

"*Sister*?" I thought.

She looked a little old to just be receiving a college degree, but I guess it's never too late to further your education. I felt bad, but still wondered how his fine ass could have the same DNA as her.

"Oh, that's nice. What college?"

"Ohio State," she responded overly proud "So *you're* Clarke? My brother mentioned you more than a few times. It isn't often that he tells *me* about a woman unless he's really interested," she smiled.

"*Really?* Did he tell you to say that?" I said blushing.

Dawn and Kenya looked clueless, but sat back attentive and taking mental notes.

"So Gregg, it was *Clarke's* shot that caught your eye?" Dawn said emphasizing my name and squinting her eyes at me.

I knew she wanted to know why he knew my real name.

"Yeah, she's got a mean shot," he smiled at me.

"Yes she does!" Kenya added sarcastically.

"So Gregg, what do you do?" Dawn asked.

"I'm a landscaper," he answered. "It's not the most exciting job, but it pays the bills," he added.

"What does a landscaper need with a gun?"

"Everyone has to protect themselves. I actually enjoy it, ya know.

"Yes, I do!" Dawn said nudging Kenya under the table and trying not to burst out in laughter.

"Oh, you shoot too?"

"A little, but not *nearly* as much as Clarke."

"Well, we really have to be going," I said interjecting, before they took the jokes too far. "It was nice to meet you Jazmine," I said shaking her hand. "*Damn she's ugly!*" I couldn't help thinking.

"Alright well, maybe I'll see you at the range. Hopefully you'll have a change of heart by then. Good evening ladies," he said tilting his head like a perfect gentleman.

"*Damn, he looks good in that suit,*" I thought as they walked off.

I placed two one hundred dollar bills on the table and I could feel the girls' eyes piercing me.

"So you know him?" Dawn asked making it obvious that she just wanted to fuck with me.

"No, you heard the man. We've met. He asked me out, that's all."

"And you said no?" she shot back with a shocked expression.

"Yes, you should try it," I said shutting the argument down.

"I feel you. My mama raised me that way too. When you find a good man, keep him a secret. Don't tell another bitch!"

I don't know why I was withholding the fact that Gregg was a job. He was really handsome and charming, but I could never date him. Before the conversation could continue, the waitress interrupted.

"Are one of you driving a Chevy Impala?" The waitress asked.

Kenya's eyes got big. "Why?"

"The alarm is going off."

We all got up and headed towards the front of the restaurant, Kenya at the head of the pack.

"My baby, what the fuck!" she yelled pulling on her braids and then throwing up her hands.

"Damn!" Dawn said adding more frustration to the situation. "See, that's why I don't fuck with bitches, too much drama," she added.

Kenya's windshield and windows were busted. All four of her tires were slashed.

"You're saying Tawnya did this?" I questioned.

I walked around to the front of the car and mouthed the words that had been scratched into her hood.

"Still watching!" Kenya mumbled.

She looked a little shaken up, but Dawn and I couldn't be there when she made the police report. I grabbed the sides of her face with my hands and looked her dead in the eyes.

"If something is wrong, tell me!" I said sincerely.

"I'm good, really. That bitch is just jealous. I'm gonna handle it. We don't need this kind of attention."

I kissed her on the forehead.

"You gonna be okay baby girl?" Dawn tried redeeming herself.

"Yeah go, go ahead."

Dawn and I got in our cars and drove off. Kenya looked around the parking lot nervously trying to case it. She called Tawnya to pick her up.

Kenya

It had been a long night, but Kenya had to get refocused. She and Dawn had a job to handle today. Robert Jackson was a twenty nine year old cable technician who'd been with his fiancé for six years and engaged to her for four. Robert wanted to add a little spice to their relationship. He asked his fiancée Nancy to consider a threesome with another woman several times. She was beginning to think he was obsessed with the idea. The very thought of it repulsed her, so compromise wasn't an option.

Having sex with two women at once seems to be at the top of every man's fantasy list, but what they don't realize is that a proposition like that can really fuck up a bitch's self-esteem and it did just that to Nancy. She began to wonder what was wrong with her and if she was satisfying him enough sexually. She tried lingerie, role-play, and even toys. None of it seemed to deter Robert's infatuation. She was in love with Robert and couldn't understand why they hadn't gotten married yet.

Robert was a big freak and she was a lot more conservative. He was into watching pornos while they fucked, particularly the videos with girl on girl action.

Robert usually took his laptop with him to work. He claimed he liked to surf the internet and check e-mails on his lunch break. That couldn't have been more untrue. One day Nancy was cleaning and realized he'd left it. She nearly killed him herself when she saw what he'd been up to. The site was called GUDKARMA.ORG. It was a website that connected ordinary people with strange or ordinary fantasies, allowing them to have encounters with one another; one night stands or ongoing.

Apparently, Robert had been searching for two women to engage in a threesome with him before he got married. In his eyes, he wouldn't *technically* be cheating. Dawn and Kenya placed an ad. They're orders were specific, kill Robert if and only if he went through with the sexual deed. If he changed his mind and his love for his fiancé outweighed his lust they were not to finish the job, but they would still be paid.

Every month the site set up a gathering of some sort for all its users. It enabled them to meet and mingle with people they'd been chatting with online. This one was held at the Renaissance Hotel, downtown.

When Kenya picked up Dawn, she could tell Dawn had been using.

"Are you up for this?"

"Shut up and drive!" Dawn replied turning up the radio and rocking her head to the music.

The party was casual. They were shocked to see that most of the people attending were kind of simple looking. Retail salesman, waitresses, people you'd never expect to have a kinky side to them.

"I'm going to go to the bathroom. You keep an eye out for him," Dawn said.

Kenya knew Dawn's trip to the bathroom had a purpose, but she spotted Robert getting a glass of wine so she approached him.

"Robert?"

He turned his head slightly and burrowed his eyebrows indicating that he had no idea who she was which was expected since Dawn and Kenya had never supplied him with a picture of them, just a lot of steamy conversation.

"It's me Connie!"

"Oh, how are you? You look good!" he said being taken back by her big almond eyes and smooth caramel skin.

"You too!" she lied.

He was average. There was an awkward moment between them.

"So where's Daina?" he asked referring to Dawn by the fake name she'd given him.

"She went to the bathroom. She said she'd be right back!"

Kenya small talked with Robert for almost twenty minutes and Dawn still hadn't surfaced.

"I'm gonna make sure she didn't fall in," she said trying to lighten up the vibe.

When she entered the bathroom, Dawn was talking to a few girls who obviously found humor in the fact she was wasted and making a fool of herself.

"Pull it together!" she said grabbing her by the arm and letting the women know the show was over. Kenya waited until they cleared out before she went in on Dawn.

"What the fuck is wrong with you? she yelled pushing her.

"You can't stay clean long enough to hit this lick? If Charlotte knew it was this bad she...."

Dawn cut her off. "Fuck Charlotte! Is Charlotte out here offing motha fuckas with us? No! That bitch is out in the suburbs sitting pretty and eating good. I guarantee you her pay check is five times more than ours is, so don't come at me with that Charlotte shit Kenya!" Dawn started to laugh. "I mean Connie!" she said stumbling a little.

Kenya grabbed her by the arm. "You're going home!"

"Like you can do this without me! Damn, will you live a little? I'm twenty six years old. I'm just trying to live!" she said yanking out of Kenya's grasp.

"Yeah, well you're doing a better job of killing yourself!" Kenya spat back out of love.

Dawn fixed her hair in the mirror, perked up her breasts, and popped a pill. "I'm ready baby!"

Kenya let out a sigh.

At the wine table, Kenya introduced Dawn to Robert as Daina. He marveled in Dawn's chinky hazel green eyes and light milky complexion.

"So we finally meet!" he said trying to shake her hand after finding himself drifting off into her cleavage.

"Cut the small talk. You know why you came here!" she whispered in his ear sloppily, almost falling over on him. He seemed uncomfortable, but he just figured she'd had a bit too much to drink.

"Well, I reserved a room upstairs if you guys want to get a little more relaxed?" he suggested.

Kenya knew exactly what he meant by *more relaxed*. Before she could answer, Dawn interrupted again. "Now, that's more like it! What's the room number?"

"Two nineteen!"

"So why don't you go get a little more comfortable, while Connie and I... damn, that's an ugly name. Connie!" Dawn cracked up losing her concentration.

"We're going to go to the gift shop," Kenya lied.

Robert retreated to the room while Dawn and Kenya went separate ways to make sure they weren't seen together.

"Pull it together!" Kenya whispered forcefully as she turned the corner.

Kenya wasted a little time in the public restroom. On the elevator ride up, she hoped desperately that Robert would make the right decision. Even though she was a full-blown lesbian, some part of her wanted to believe that there were still a few decent men around, plus she had no problem having one less body on her gun and still getting paid for it.

When she arrived at the room, the door was cracked and it creaked slightly as she pushed it. She wasn't surprised to see Dawn completely naked and undressing Robert. She grew uncomfortable and sat in a chair across the room. She watched Dawn seduce him as she kissed on his neck and then the head of his dick. Kenya dropped the box of condoms startling them and they both looked up.

"You two seem to be getting along just fine without me!" she said regretting excepting the job.

"Come here," Dawn, said seductively.

As Kenya approached the bed, Dawn stood to her feet and slid Kenya's jacket off of her shoulders slowly. Robert positioned himself at the top of the bed where he could get a clear view of the both of them. Dawn guided Kenya to a sitting position at the foot of the bed and sat behind her with her legs wide open and he breast pressed against Kenya's back. She pulled all of Kenya's braids onto one of her shoulders and pulled her shirt over her head. Kenya's eyes were locked on the floor, so Dawn couldn't see her facial expression. She hadn't made a sound so Dawn assumed she was into it.

Robert looked on, his manhood throbbing as Dawn popped Kenya's bra open in one smooth motion. Most *men* hadn't mastered that maneuver. He let out a moan and began stroking himself. Kenya's body grew tense as Dawn kissed up her back and neck while seducing Robert in the mirror with her cat eyes.

Suddenly, Dawn stopped and Kenya came back to earth.

"Aren't you going to join the party big daddy?" she said pressuring him to make a move so she could let him have it.

Kenya could tell Dawn was getting agitated."Maybe he wasn't going to go through with it," she thought. "Maybe he really did love his girl and was having second thoughts."

"I think I'll watch for a while," he said sounding a bit nervous.

"So, you came all the way here to watch?" Dawn asked growing more impatient.

"Calm down. He's just not comfortable," Kenya, said trying to lighten the mood.

"Yeah, I'm just a little nervous that's all," Robert sided with Kenya.

"Nervous? Oh, now you're nervous? Were you nervous when you got your sick ass online looking for two '*down for whatever bitches*'?"

Kenya knew the drugs in Dawn's system had reached their full potency as Dawn approached him waving her index finger and then pressing it into his chest.

"Were you nervous when you lied to your fiancé about where you were going to be tonight?"

The look on Robert's face made it obvious he was no longer turned on in any way and that the sudden change in the mood would probably never recover.

"Can I talk to you for a minute?" Kenya said snatching Dawn up by the arm. "Excuse us!" she said pulling her into the bathroom.

She turned on the water in the sink."Keep it up and were leaving!" Kenya whispered forcefully.

"You liked it!" Dawn said leaning in sloppily and licking Kenya on the cheek.

Before she knew it, she'd grabbed Dawn by the throat and hemmed her up against the wall. "Don't test me! I'm not going to keep covering for you. The deal was to handle him if he participated and you know he wasn't gonna do it. So stop pushing him. You got me?" She released her grasp roughly.

"I got you!" Dawn replied with a gleam in her eye.

Kenya reached in her pocket and handed Dawn the keys to the rental.

"What's this?"

"Go to the car, I'm going to finish the job."

Dawn started to laugh."Yeah right! Sure you are," she said as she walked out of the bathroom and headed towards the car. Kenya took a deep breath. When she walked back in the room Robert was fully dressed and zipping his coat.

"Look I'm really sorry!" he said genuinely. "I should have never come here. Maybe this is a sign ya know. Maybe I need to work things out with Nancy."

Kenya smiled on the inside realizing her intuition about him was right as he left the room. She waited about five minutes before leaving the room to join Dawn in the car. She got in and started the engine.

"So?"

"So what?"

"You didn't do it. Did you?"

"Yes, I took care of it."

"Then call Charlotte!" Dawn challenged her.

Kenya hesitated. "He wasn't gonna do it."

"I knew it. You're getting soft!"

She pulled off. Dawn antagonized Kenya the entire way home. When they pulled up in front of her loft, her high had come down a bit. Kenya pushed the unlock button, but didn't part her lips and her eyes remained fixated on the road ahead.

"Be honest, you wanted me didn't you?"Dawn taunted caressing Kenya's thigh.

Kenya slapped her hand away, walked around to the passenger side, and opened the door. "Get out the damn car!" she insisted.

"What's wrong? I'm not your type?" she said sarcastically, batting her eyes.

"Just because I like women doesn't mean I like all women! I have standards!" Kenya fired back.

Dawn became infuriated. The thought of anyone rejecting her left a bad taste in her mouth. She thought of the most evil thing she could say to Kenya to get the last word.

"So your stepdad could touch you, but I can't huh?" she fired knowing her comment would cut deep.

Kenya yanked Dawn out the car and onto the cement.

"That's it. I'm done. You're a spoiled ass brat! You have no fuckin idea what it's like not to be able to turn to your own mother for help; for your own mother to turn her back on you and call you a liar! You're a waste Dawn, a motha fuckin waste!"

Kenya's mom knew of her sexual abuse, but never did anything to combat it. She saw it as the only way to keep her man and the one time Kenya tried to confess, she threatened to disown her if she ever mentioned it to anyone. Dawn was the only person Kenya had ever confided in about the horrible details of her sexual abuse.

Kenya slammed the door and pulled off leaving Dawn on her ass in the middle of the street. They'd had their sisterly spats before, but Dawn had never seen her so upset and wondered if maybe she'd pushed it a little too far.

Clarke

It had been a couple weeks since I'd talked to either of the girls, but I was sure that the both of them had already put their plans into motion by now. I on the other hand, hadn't been to the range or classes and was long overdue to let off some steam.

"Hey Bob," I said throwing my hand up at the manager and heading to my usual lane.

Before I could even finish loading up, I felt the presence of someone standing behind me, *thanks to my inner chi classes*. I didn't need to turn to know who. I continued to load.

"How can I help you Mr. Thomas?" I said aggravated.

"Change your mind yet?"

"You know, this could be considered stalking even borderline sexual harassment!" I snapped. "And as I told you Mr. Thomas..."

"Gregg, call me Gregg," he interrupted.

"As I told you before *Mr. Thomas*, I don't do dinner!" I said putting on my protective eyewear.

"Now I'm confused Clarke. Did I not see you out to dinner with two of your friends? So what exactly does, *you don't do dinner* mean?" he asked mocking me.

The fact that he knew my real name was really starting to bother me. "It means that I've been to every five star restaurant in Cleveland, so I'm not interested in you taking me somewhere I can obviously pay for myself," I said as bitchy as possible adding a little neck roll and crossing my arms.

"Five star? I was thinking something more like KFC."

My stomach felt queasy just from the thought of it. "Fast food for a fast guy!" I poked.

He laughed. "I know who you are Clarke!"

I switched my weight to my other hip and tightened my lips. "You don't know shit about me!"

"What did he do?"

"Who?"

"Whoever hurt you. You're not this tough girl you're trying to portray. How about this Friday? I promise to take you to eat somewhere nice, somewhere you've never been. The food will be delicious and the

70

service will be incredible! If I'm wrong, I won't bother you anymore. Deal?" he said extending his hand for a shake.

My mind wondered back to Charlotte, and how she said a job was a job. "So you'll leave me alone?" I said unconvinced.

"My word is my bond," he smiled with that perfect smile, not realizing he had just sealed his fate...

"Fine, *216-299-5188.* Do not call me before noon, let your number show, and if I don't answer, I'll call *you* back. Don't overdo it!" I said sharply.

He was still smiling."Friday," he said.

I raised my nine millimeter and took aim down my lane.

"You know, if you bring that right elbow in a little, your shot will be a lot more accurate."

I smacked my lips because I knew I had a crazy shot and so did he. As Gregg walked away, I pulled my right elbow in and fired a bullet. It went straight through the X on the mannequin's heart. I smiled.

Kenya

Tawnya grabbed the back of Kenya's head and pushed it deep between her legs as her body jerked while she climaxed. Tawnya's legs went limp and her head fell back on the pillow. Kenya laid next to her stroking her hair while she caught her breath. Finally, Tawnya interrupted her panting.

"When are you going to stop lying to me?"

"Lying? Lying about what?" Kenya lashed back.

"Keeping a secret is the same thing as lying," she turned over and looked at her with attitude. "Are you fucking a nigga?"

Kenya exploded with laughter. "Be for real!"

"So then what's funny? First it was your face, then the store, and what the hell happened to your car?"

"I'm not gonna do this right now Tawnya!"Kenya tried avoiding the conversation.

"So then when are we gonna do this?"

Tawnya was preparing to let Kenya have it, when a loud banging on the front door interrupted their argument. They both got quiet, looked at the door, and then looked at each other.

"I'll get it!" Kenya said jumping up and grabbing her gun.

She looked out the peephole and saw nothing.

"Who is it?"

There was no response. She heard tires peel off. She opened the door and didn't see anyone. She looked around then stepped out onto the porch barefoot.

"Shit!" she yelled grabbing the bottom of her foot.

She'd stepped on something. Her mouth hung open when she realized what it was a single bullet from a sawed off shotgun.

"Who is it?" Tawnya called out.

"Just some bad ass kids," she said locking all three locks.

Chapter 4

Old Dog New Tricks

Dawn

It was 9:00 PM, the time Quincy Morgan usually hit the strip. Dawn stood on the corner of East 22nd and Prospect. Men dressed as women gave her hard stares as if to say; *what are you doing in our territory?* Dawn was wearing a blonde wig, shades, a tank top, and mini skirt with no underwear. Her patience was getting short. She'd been waiting almost thirty minutes and the cold of the fall night was beginning to raise chill bumps on her arms and legs. Finally a cream Honda Civic passed by. She looked at the license plate.

"Mr. Morgan!" she whispered.

The Civic slowed as it passed and turned the corner. She thought he wasn't interested until she noticed that he'd stopped and turned his lights off. She approached the car from the passenger side and tried to get in, but it was locked. Quincy rolled down the window. He looked every bit of his age. There wasn't a strand of black hair on his entire head. He looked over his glasses and asked, "You hot?" attempting to make sure she wasn't undercover. He spoke dryly as though he had done this many times before.

"What are you looking for?"

"Oral, maybe little fucking!" He was old school. "How many roses you want for that?" he asked still not completely secure with Dawn, seeing as how he'd never seen her on the strip.

"Fifty," Dawn responded thinking that was a low price, but probably average for a prostitute. "Let's get off the street!" she added trying to convince him she was legitimate.

"Fifty?" he chuckled. "Please, you're not that cute hun and a little lighter than I like them. I prefer my chocolate dark!"

Dawn was pissed and her patience was getting shorter. She felt like a real hoe standing outside of this man's car door, which she was, but she wasn't into letting other people make her feel that way.

"Well, neither are you pops!" she snapped back.

He looked shocked, but somewhat turned on. "Alright mulatto, I'll give you a shot, but for thirty," he said unlocking the door.

Dawn rolled her eyes and hopped in.

"Where to?" he asked.

"There's a YMCA a few blocks down. The parking lot is always empty."

Quincy started to unbutton his pants with his free hand as he drove. When they parked, he began stroking himself.

"In a rush?" Dawn joked.

"Make sure you pull the skin back!" he instructed her.

He was uncircumcised. His wrinkled sagging skin was a complete turn off, but Dawn had dealt with worse. She leaned over and pulled the skin back on his penis. It looked like raw ground beef. She began to give him oral sex. For an old guy Quincy was hanging in there. Dawn had had enough of the games. She climbed on top of him in the driver seat and began to fuck the old bag raw, skin to skin. His moans were weak and uninviting. His eyes closed as his wrinkled hands grabbed her waste. She reached and grabbed her short and sleek Bowie hunting knife out of her bra and jabbed it into his neck piercing his jugular. Blood leaked down the front of his clothes. She twisted it and then pulled the knife out to ensure maximum blood flow. Then she waited a while. When she felt his once erect penis go limp inside of her and she knew immediately he was dead. Dawn reached into his pocket and pulled out his wallet.

"Five hundred dollars! You cheap fuck!" she exclaimed stuffing the money in her bra.

She stepped out the driver's side, did a double check for any evidence, took off her shirt, threw it in her bag, and walked naturally through the parking lot while reaching for her phone to call Charlotte.

Clarke

Friday seemed to arrive in a blink of an eye. It was five minutes till six and I'd agreed to meet Gregg at his house by six, so I knew I'd be late. Two wardrobe changes and I still weren't satisfied.

Gregg told me to dress casual. My authentic Dereon jeans hugged my curves and my eight hundred dollar Louis Vuitton boots matched my lightweight suit jacket, perfect for the fall weather. I grabbed the directions I'd written down off my dresser and hopped in my truck. I took Route 2 until it ended on the city's Westside. When I turned onto Gregg's street the car behind me honked its horn due to my slow pace. The houses on his street were so beautiful. I was too busy admiring them to realize that I was only driving about five miles an hour.

"3391, 3395, 3397," I said aloud reading the addresses and glancing down at the directions.

I made a right into the driveway that was supposed to be Gregg's. It was a gorgeous colonial style, all white, two-floor home that sat off the Lake.

"This can't be right!" I mumbled to myself.

I flipped open my phone and dialed Gregg."Hello."

"*Damn he sounds sexy,*" I thought. It had been a while since a man's voice had been so invigorating to me. "Hey, it's me."

"Hey beautiful. Having trouble finding the place?"

"Well, I'm on Edgewater. I think I got a little turned around though. What did you say the address was again?" I said looking at the paper, then at the numbers on the house again.

"3397. Where are you?"

"I guess I'm outside."

"Okay, I'll be right down."

I tapped my fingers on the steering wheel and checked my hair quickly in the mirror. Shortly after, Gregg came down. He looked amazing. I could tell he'd gotten his hair line touched up. He walked up to the car door.

"So are you gonna get out?" he said tapping on the window.

I rolled my eyes. "I thought we were going out?" I said hesitating to open the door.

"No I never said that! I said I could take you somewhere nice to eat you'd never been. You really need to learn to relax. Not everyone is out to get you," he said taking me by the hand.

We walked up his long driveway.

"So what did you say you do again?" I asked admiring his house.

"I'm a landscaper," he said confidently.

I started laughing.

"What?"

"Nothing. You just don't strike me as a gardener and a gardener with a gun at that. Doesn't seem like a very exciting career, that's all."

"Well, I enjoy it."

"These are pretty comfortable living arrangements for a landscaper," I joked.

"Yeah, I make due," he said smiling with that gorgeous smile.

There was a short trail down the side of house that appeared to lead to a garden of some sort.

"This doesn't look like dinner," I said giving a little attitude.

"Relax. You're in good hands. Besides, I've seen your shot. If I get out of line, I know you wouldn't hesitate to take me out!" he said trying to suppress my anxiety.

I liked that fact that Gregg acknowledged me being a strong woman and wasn't turned off by it, but little did he know the truth in his sarcasm. When we were almost to the end of the trail, he stepped in my path and looked me in the face.

"Close your eyes."

The combination of my trust issues and killer instincts made me reluctant, but there was something about Gregg that made me feel so comfortable no matter how hard I tried to fight it. I closed my eyes. He led me further down the trail. When we stopped he put both hands around my waste and said, "Open them."

I hesitated and opened them one at a time. I was speechless. He'd set up a table under a tree that overlooked the entire city and the lake. Two silver plates with lids sat on a white satin tablecloth. Flower pedals and candles showed that he'd put a lot of thought into it.

"It's beautiful!" I said breaking my silence.

"Not as much as you," he replied sincerely.

He pulled out my chair for me and uncovered my food. It was a chicken dinner from KFC. Tears ran down my face from laughing so hard.

"What?" he laughed along with me?

"*This is so cute!*" I thought to myself.

"It's not about what you eat, but who you share it with. Besides I'm not much of a cook, breakfast is my specialty," he said taking his seat across from me.

"What makes you think I'll be here for breakfast?" I joked.

"Wishful thinking I guess. So, tell me more about you."

"Like what?"

"I don't know. What's you favorite color?"

"Turquoise."

"When's your birthday?"

80

"September nineteenth."

"Oh, that's in few weeks. How old will you be?"

"You never ask a lady her age!" I smiled.

"I see you're not going to make this easy for me. So where do you work?"

"Newman, Margiano, and Jones Law Firm. I'm a legal secretary."

"Oh, that explains it!" he said nodding his head several times and taking a sip of his drink.

"Explains what?"

"You're around people that lie all day!"

We both smiled. We talked and joked for hours. By eleven, I had to be getting home, so he walked me to my car.

"So I guess this means I get a second date!"

"I'm sorry?" I said knowing I had every intention of seeing him again.

"I won the bet," he said brushing my auburn tresses off my face.

"But you cheated," I said getting a little squeamish because he was so close.

He sent chills down my body as he leaned in for a kiss. I stared into his eyes and began to move closer allowing my eyelids to slowly close.

Just as our lips were about to touch, a vibrating sensation startled me, forcing my eyes to open.

"That's just my pager," he said closing his eyes trying to capture the mood again.

"Who the fuck still uses a pager anymore?" I thought completely annoyed.

"I gotta go Gregg. I'll call you," I said uncomfortably while scrambling for my car keys.

"Wait, I'm really sorry," he said reaching in his pocket to turn it off.

I got in the car and backed all the way out his long driveway.

"Clarke, wait!" he said throwing his hands up.

"I'll call you!" I yelled out the window.

When I reached the end of the street, I stopped and hit my hands on the steering wheel.

"Damn it Clarke! Never fall for a hit!" I said frustrated with myself. My phone interrupted my thoughts. I looked at the caller I.D. hoping it wasn't Gregg. "What's up lil mama?" It was Kenya.

"Clarke, I can't do this anymore! I want out! I can't do this shit no more!" her toned inclined.

"Wait, slow down. Think about what you're doing. You know this is against the rules. Whatever it is we'll work it out when I see in a few weeks. Pull yourself together!" I demanded.

This was really out of pocket for Kenya.

"They wanna kill me!" she screamed. "Is this payback for all the lives I took? Oh, God they're gonna kill me!"

I could tell she was crying hysterically because she could barely catch her breath. There was nothing I could do at this point. She knew it was completely against our rules to talk this way over the phone.

"I'll see you soon," I said and closed my phone.

The tone in her voice had struck a nerve. I knew it was best not to act hasty, but my motherly instincts forced me to drive by her house a few times.

Kenya

Kenya's nerves were shot. She had become extremely paranoid, thinking that everyone was out to get her. She got in her car without saying a word to Tawnya and took off. She began to do something she hadn't done in a long time. Pray.

"Jehovah, I know I haven't been the best person, in my life, I know I just..." Her sentences were fragmented and confusing. "You see me go down there every Saturday and talk to those kids about not making the same mistakes I did. You see me trying to make it right!" she yelled.

Her foot got heavy on the gas. She sped through the streets like a mental patient with a death wish.

Kenya grew up in a home that strictly abided by Jehovah's Witness teachings. Her mother was very submissive when it came to her husband. Kenya was taught that the man's orders were not debatable and that questioning or accusing her parents of sin would send her to a firey eternity in hell. When Kenya finally mustered up the strength to tell her mother she was being molested by her step dad, she was immediately silenced. Her mother told her that the Bible teaches children to honor and obey their parents.

Kenya spent many nights curled up in the dark corners of her room, afraid the devil would come to confiscate her for being "disobedient", as her mother called it. She suffered for years at the touch of her step dad, until she developed enough courage to run away from home.

After the murder of her step dad, she tried once more to rekindle her relationship with her estranged mother, but she wanted nothing to do with Kenya and disowned her when she found out she was gay.

As Kenya raced through the dark streets, her hands became clammy and her forehead filled with beads of sweat. When the car finally stopped, she found herself in a place she hadn't been since she was a child. The Kingdom Hall was a place of congregation in the Jehovah's Witness religion.

It was late so the doors were locked. She threw herself on the stairs and began to sob uncontrollably.

"I'm sorry, I'm so sorry!" she repeated over and over again, weeping more with each apology.

Kenya hadn't been to the Kingdom Hall, a church, or any place of worship for that matter in years. She hadn't so much as lowered her head to recite a prayer over a meal. Her life situations had forced her to lose all faith she had in God. Though she hadn't been exactly living by the Ten Commandments, she was the most compassionate of the girls. For a brief moment, she felt a feeling of peace come over her, but it was quickly interrupted when two bright headlights shining from an all white unmarked van blinded her eyesight. She stood up figuring it was just security or someone who worked for the Kingdom Hall. Two men walked towards her.

"I was just leaving," she said holding her forearm over her eyes to try and make out their faces.

Her eyes were red and swollen and the light made them even more sensitive. She bent down to grab her keys.

"I told you I was watching you!" she heard one of them say.

She turned and saw that both of the men were wearing ski masks. She tried to scurry up the steps, but one of them grabbed her ankle and pulled her towards him, scraping her face on the concrete.

"Get her arms!" one instructed the other.

She kicked her legs and whaled her arms, fighting as hard as she could. For a second she got a few feet away, but they recaptured her and threw her in the back of the van. They gagged her and tied her legs and arms behind her back. After checking to make sure the knots were secure, they both hopped in the front of the van and took off.

The two-hour ride drained all of her energy as she bounced around in the back of the van with no way to protect her head from injury. She felt the road become more turbulent as they made the switch from pavement to gravel. The van came to a sudden stop and she felt both doors slam shut almost simultaneously. The kidnappers opened the back doors and carried her weak body into a shed.

"Right here," one of them said.

She looked up trying to open her eyes, but they were having trouble adjusting due to being in the dark van for so long. When she finally gained her sight, she saw that they were still wearing their ski masks. If they had planned on killing her, their identities would have no longer needed to be concealed. One of them seemed gittery and nervous. The other was more relaxed and seemed to dominate the other. Kenya thought she recognized his voice from the shop a few months ago.

He grabbed her by the chin and looked her in the eyes.

"You almost shot me!" he said confirming her speculation as he pointed to a burn mark on his neck.

The other kidnapper just looked on. Kenya began to ponder their intensions. It couldn't have been for ransom. No one knew of her involvement with the girls.

"All this over a connect?" she thought.

"She looks sick. Maybe we should drop her off at a hospital," the nervous one said. He obviously wasn't a killer.

"A hospital? Are you fucking crazy! Go to the van and get me some water!"

Kenya and the man eyed each other. Her lids got heavy again and she closed them as she laid still bound on a dirty blanket. He pulled a pocketknife from a bag and cut open her shirt. He sliced her bra straps exposing her breasts. She laid there unable to retaliate.

"Hey, I didn't see any water!"

The second kidnapper stopped in his tracks. "What are you doing? You said we were just going to scare her. I'm down with that perverted shit man! I'm leaving. You can keep your money," he said taking off.

The remaining kidnapper unzipped his pants and pulled his dick out. "I told you, I was gonna give you some of this dick!"

He got down on the blanket with her and cut a hole in her sweat pants exposing her pussy. He ripped the hole with both hands to make it bigger. He stuck his face in her crotch and inhaled deeply. Then he climbed on top of her. She couldn't move or scream so she just glared into his eyes trying to make them speak to him, trying to pierce his soul with compassion. He merely turned her head away and shoved himself into her dry vagina, moaning and groaning as though the situation were normal.

"Yeah, you like this dick don't you? You little gay bitch! You like it don't you!"

Kenya was exhausted. She didn't even drop a tear. When he was finished he came inside of her and tried to drip was left onto her face. He redressed and cut her hands free, but she didn't budge. Shortly after he left the shed, she heard the van pulling off and speeding through the gravel.

She laid on the floor of the shed for two days, wishing she'd just die. Halfway through the third day, she forced herself to get up; not because she believed, God would give her the strength to heal and not because she knew holding on was the right thing to do. Kenya had one thing on her mind and that was revenge. She hitchhiked back to town and cleaned up at a motel. As she soaked in the tub, she lost all compassion for the world and everything in it. She planned to contact a few friends who had the hook up on some serious ammunition. She was gonna have something for his ass if he was brave enough to strike again. She snatched the crucifix necklace her mother had given her from her neck and threw it at the wall. Hate filled her heart.

Clarke

Almost two weeks had passed since I talked to Gregg. I was avoiding all of his calls and hadn't been to the range since our date. I didn't know what the hell was wrong with me, but I knew I needed to shake it quick. Bottom line, he was a job and if Charlotte found out about my hesitation, she would not be pleased. I sat at my desk tapping my pen and staring at the phone while I figured out what I was going to say to him. The phone rang making that decision for me.

"Newman, Margiano, and Jones Law Firm, is this call in reference to representation?"

"Happy Birthday Clarke."

"Hello?" I said trying to pretend I didn't know it was Gregg.

"I'm sorry to call you on your job, but you weren't exactly returning my calls. Did I do something wrong?"

"No, not at all. I've just been really busy, I lied.

"Sure you have," he laughed and I pictured the dimple in his right cheek.

"So how did you get this number?"

"Phonebook. It is listed," he said brushing it off. "You're nineteen today right?" he said trying to flatter me, but really offending me.

"Thirty," I said dryly. I was the oldest of the girls and felt like it.

Where had time gone?

"Ms. Williams?" a voice said interrupting my thoughts.

"Yes," I said tucking the phone under my chin and looking to see who it was.

"There's a delivery for you," my coworker informed me.

"Hold on a second Gregg," I said putting him on hold.

"Tell them to bring it in."

When I got up from my seat I was greeted by a huge bouquet of turquoise flowers that nearly made the delivery boy invisible.

"Thank you," I said admiring them as I signed.

"Blaue Blumes are one the rarest flowers in the world. They had to be shipped in from Germany. It's the country's symbol of love and desire. You must be a special girl," he said smiling.

I blushed and took a long whiff of the flowers. "Guess so huh?"

"Take care," he said.

"I love them," I said taking the phone off hold.

"Anything for you Ms. Williams," he said slyly indicating that he knew I'd been lying about my last name. "So can I see you tonight?" he said taking advantage of my gratitude.

I paused because everything in me knew I was running out of time to handle the job, but it wasn't exactly my first priority. "Yeah, sure," I said.

"How about Constantino's? It's Italian," he said.

"I know," I bragged. "How about my place?" I blurted out even shocking myself. It had been a while since a man had been over to my place.

"Are you sure?" he said sounding bewildered.

"*God he's perfect*," I thought "Yea, how about eight?"

"Eight it is Ms. Williams."

We hung up. Gregg was sweet, but I was hoping he wasn't going to turn out to be one of those stalker types, mysteriously showing up where ever I went.

Chapter 5

Business and Pleasure

Kenya

Kenya was still on pins and needles. She and Tawnya had grown more distant due to the fact that she wasn't sharing what was bothering her. She parked in front of her house and saw Tawnya frantically throwing her clothes on the front lawn in a big pile. Kenya was very particular when it came to the kind of clothes she wore. People knew she was always dressed to impress and that's why she had frequent customers. Watching her expensive wardrobe being thrown in the dirt was enough to send her off the deep end.

"What is wrong with you?"she yelled neglecting to even close the car door behind her.

"Who is she?" Tawnya screamed dropping another load of clothes on the lawn.

"How the fuck can you put me out of my own damn house? Girl, you betta pick this shit up and take it back inside. I don't have time for this."

"I said who is she!" Tawnya yelled louder as she lifted a gas can from the porch and motioned to douse Kenya's things.

Kenya eyeballed her. "You better..."

Tawnya popped the top off the can, silencing Kenya for a moment.

"Who is who?"

"The bitch in the silver Ferrari!"

Kenya knew Tawnya was describing my car. She must have seen me when I drove by a few times to check for Kenya's car.

"Brown skin, long hair. Oh, you don't know? I got the bitch's license plate number!"

"Look, I got some business to take care of and I sware to God when I get back all of this shit better be back in my motha fucking house!"

By now, a few of the neighbors had congregated outside. Kenya and Tawnya argued on a regular basis. No one bothered to call the police anymore. Instead, they enjoyed the entertainment.

"You always gotta handle some damn business! You selling drugs again aren't you? I'm not going to be with a fuckin dope girl Kenya!"

Even with as much drama as Tawnya brought to the table, Kenya loved her and knew the feeling was mutual.

"Get my shit in the house," Kenya said heading for the car.

"Where are you going?" Tawna followed more concerned than upset.

Kenya started up the car and rolled up her window. Tawnya hit the door and kicked the tire just as it pulled off.

"I hate you Kenya!" she hollered, knowing she was lying. She looked up finally realizing she had an audience. "What the fuck are yall looking at?"She began to pick the clothes off the ground and take Kenya's things back into the house.

Kenya waited in a rental car in front of a Gyro shop on East Fifty Fifth Street and St. Clair. She was suppose to meet with Tone, a good friend of hers and confidant when she was in the game. He sort of took over things when she left the street life. Tone was heavy in the hood, so if anybody knew the word around town, it was him. She was hoping he could point her in the direction of any niggas planning to do her greasy. He also had the connect on some heavy artillery and Kenya loved exclusive heat. Soon Tone pulled up alongside her.

"Hop in."

Kenya jumped in the passenger seat and he pulled into an alley just a few blocks down the street.

"What's up baby?" he said slapping hands with her and then embracing her.

"Those twenty six inch rims. That's what's up!" she laughed."I see you still out here drawing extra attention to yourself."

"Twenty eight inches!" he corrected her. "And fuck the police. So, what's good? You know if anybody got a problem with Killa K, then they got a problem with me!" he said seriously.

"I've been getting a lot of threats lately. Kinda got me shook. I was wondering if you knew anything about it."

"Threats? What kind of threats? You know if I heard anything like that it would already be a few bodies face down in the dirt!"

"I know." Kenya felt a little more secure. "Just keep your ears open for me alright!"

"Anything for you baby girl. You know that." They embraced once more.

"So whatchu' got for me?" she asked.

Tone reached into his back seat and pulled out a black suitcase. Inside were three hand guns.

"Whatchu' know about that? That's exclusive shit right there!" he bragged.

Kenya's eyes were immediately drawn to the silver Beretta PX4 Storm, built with a rounded trigger guard for better concealed carry.

"Now that's my style!" she said picking it up and peering down the top of it with one eye closed as she took aim at a pretend target.

"You sure you can handle that?"

"Could you handle it!" she laughed cocking it back and looking in the chamber to make sure it was empty.

"Well, that one is on me!"

"Thanks. Good looking out!"she smiled putting it in her bag.

"So what else has been up, besides niggas trying to punk you?"

"Shit, making an honest living."

"Making an honest living ain't gonna buy you guns like that. Your pockets straight? I heard you selling clothes and shit!" he teased her reaching in the glove compartment and pulling out a thick stack of cash.

"Yeah, I'm good."

"You sure?" he insisted pulling off about two thousand dollars in fifties and shoving it her way.

"I'm good really!" she refused.

"Baby girl, take this money!" he said forcing it into her hands.

Before Kenya could thank him, she felt a cold rush of air and glass fly across her face.

"Put your fucking hands on the dash bitch!" a young thug in a ski mask demanded.

"Give me the money! Give me the God damn money!" another one on the driver side yelled at Tone.

Kenya's heart pounded as she experienced what it was like to be on the other side of the barrel. "Just give him the money Tone!" she signaled with her hands.

"I said keep your hands on the dash!"

She felt a blow from the handle of the gun against her head. Tone thought this was a big enough distraction and tried reaching for his gun. Shots echoed! Kenya felt five surges of heat pierce through her body two in her left leg, one in her stomach, and two in her chest. The pain was too excruciating to even scream for help. She looked over at Tone, whose body was limp and lifeless as the second robber snatched the cash from his hand and took off.

Kenya's quest for revenge had just placed her in the wrong place at the wrong time. Blood seeped from her mouth as she blacked in and out of consciousness. She heard no police, no ambulance, and no pedestrians. She thought of Rick, her step dad, and all the men she'd killed in her lifetime. She knew that this was it and God would make her lay there suffering and slowly bleeding to death as her punishment. She reached down mustering up all the energy she had left in her body and cocked back her Smith and Wesson. She pressed the barrel up against her temple and took a deep breath with her eyes squeezed shut.

"If anybody's gonna take me out of this world it's me!"

She pulled the trigger. Exactly forty nine seconds after Kenya took her own life a medical EMT pressed his fingers against her wrist to feel for a pulse. He signaled to his partner.

"She's gone."

Clarke

I was getting ready for a night of ecstasy with Gregg. After all the work he had been putting in, he deserved it. Hell, I deserved it. It had been months. I had prepared dinner and dimmed the lighting. Just as I was giving myself, one last glance over in the mirror the door bell rang. I looked at the clock. It was 7:59.

"*Damn he's good,*" I thought.

I opened the door and he was standing there with a bottle of wine and a box of chocolates in hand.

"You look beautiful as usual;" he complimented me in my form fitting all black strapless Armani dress.

"Likewise," I said returning the favor.

I liked Gregg because he was classy; the kind of guy you could take home to mom and not be ashamed to take to a fancy place, not to mention easy to look at. Our smooth brown skin went well together. He hugged me.

"These are for you!" he said.

"Thank you. Have a seat. I'll take your jacket."

Honestly, at this point I couldn't have cared less about dinner or what intellectual conversation he had to offer. I wanted him bad. I popped open the wine. It was Pinot Grigio, my favorite. We sat down on the couch and conversed for a while. Don't ask me about what! I was too busy being mesmerized by his lips to pay attention to anything else.

"Don't you think so?" he asked.

"Yeah, definitely!" I agreed having no idea what he'd just said.

He laughed. Our eyes met and finally so did our lips. They were so soft and passionate. He ran his fingers through the back of my hair. His touch was gentle yet still so manly. This *Jason's Lyric* shit was cute, but I didn't want to waste anymore time. Hell, he had me from hello. I kissed him harder moaning and breathing heavily in his ear to let him know I was ready. We kissed and touched our way all the way to my bedroom. Then suddenly he stopped.

"What's wrong?" I asked panting.

He hesitated before answering. "Clarke, I'm not looking for a quick fix. I like you, a lot."

I started to kiss his neck trying to get him back in the mood.

"I like you too baby," I said obviously yearning for his touch.

In one smooth motion, he lifted me clear off the floor and laid me on my back. This aggressive behavior was a real turn on to me, especially since I'd never met a man who could handle my toughness. He began to massage my shoulders. He kissed every part of my body from my lips to the tips of my toes and I mean every part. His lips weren't dry or too wet. They stuck to my skin a little right before he'd pull them away. Perfect. When he entered me, I exhaled and sank my fingers into his back. My kegel muscles throbbed as his big dick filled my pussy from wall to wall. His shoulder blades danced around under his skin as he dug into me slowly until I almost climaxed. Luckily the room was dimly lit. For that, I was thankful. Thankful he couldn't see my pupils filling up with water, forming massive tears, and then cascading down my pronounced cheeks bones. I'd never felt so open, so vulnerable, so much like a woman coy and submissive. Every emotion God had given his delicate creature was pulsating through my limbs, racing through my bones. I got swept away by the symphony of sound his groaning, my moaning, and our breathing. He took his hand and wiped away years of pain as he dried my eyes. He dug deeper inside of me and a few tears became a river accompanied by a whimper. It was so good, I cried. I was slightly embarrassed, but I wasn't in pain. I was in love.

Just when I thought I couldn't take anymore, he pulled out and licked my pussy as though there were a hidden treasure deep within it. My entire body started to shake uncontrollably.

Once again, he made me speechless and I'm rarely speechless! He laid my head on his chest and caressed my hair. No one had ever put it on me like this before. I was used to men who made you do all the work and then took all the credit. I fell asleep in his arms.

In the morning, I awoke to an empty bed, but somehow I wasn't surprised. Up until this point Gregg had been everything, I ever hoped for in a man and more. No one could be flawless. I would have never pegged him for a one night stand though. Just as I was coming to grips with the fact that I'd probably never see him again, I caught wind of a smell I hadn't smelled in years, breakfast! Gregg entered the room with a plate and a glass of orange juice. He sat down on the edge of the bed shirtless. I was still naked so I covered my breasts with the sheets and sat up.

"You're just as beautiful in the morning!" he said smiling.

"Good morning," I smiled back. "*And that it is.*" I thought.

"I told you breakfast was my specialty!"

Breakfast wasn't the only thing he specialized in. He'd made toast, eggs, bacon, and hash browns.

"Where did you get this?" I asked knowing my refrigerator had the bare necessities water, ice cream, and a few microwaveable dinners. It was a mystery to me how I maintained my figure.

"I went out."

At that moment, I gave up on trying to find a flaw in him.

"You gonna feed me?" I asked seductively.

He proceeded to do just that.

"*This is the best breakfast I've ever had!*" I thought to myself and I'm sure it was written all over my face. As I slipped off into pure euphoria, that damn pager went off again, breaking the mood.

"Sorry, can I use your phone? Mine is dead."

"Yeah it's in the kitchen."

When he returned I'd almost finished eating. "What's wrong?" I asked due to the fact that he seemed a little hasty.

"Don't be upset, but I' have to run." "Alright well handle your business. Just call me later," I said trying not to look too disappointed as I watched him quickly dress.

"*Déjà vu,*" I thought.

A few months ago if any other man had been in such a hurry to leave after a long night of love making I would have been suspicious immediately, but I knew Gregg's feelings for me were sincere. He kissed me on the forehead and then on the lips. As I watched him pull off I heard my cell phone ringing in the bedroom and I raced to catch it.

"Miss me already?" I asked assuming Gregg felt terrible for leaving so soon.

"What?" Dawn answered. "You need to get down here. They didn't resuscitate her. They didn't even try!" she yelled.

"Who? What are you talking about?"

"Kenya!" she sobbed.

I felt like someone had just hit me with a semi truck. "Where are you?" I barely whispered.

"Lutheran Hospital."

I dropped the phone and raced to throw on the first thing I saw.

"Hello? Hello? Clarke!" Dawn yelled into the receiver.

The speed limit was the furthest thing from my mind as I did ninety miles per hour through residential areas. Kenya's voice echoed in my mind. I felt terrible for not listening to her when she needed me. As I approached the hospital, I prayed that somehow Kenya was okay and that this was just a really bad dream that I was going to wake up from any minute. When I pulled up, I thought I saw Gregg's truck, but I was too broken up to know for sure. I rushed to the E.R. department. A nurse jumped in front of me.

"Miss, can I help you?"

"Get the fuck out of my way!" I shouted letting her know I meant business.

I could hear her calling for security as I ran down the hallway looking from room to room frantically. I saw a sign that said morgue with an arrow pointing down. The elevator seemed to take forever so I ran down the stairs. As soon as I turned the corner, I saw Dawn standing in the hallway pacing and holding her mouth. I pushed open the door and they were zipping Kenya's body bag. I started to vomit instantly.

"You can't be in here!" the security guard said firmly.

I wanted to cry, but nothing would come out. I felt my knees get weak before I fell to the floor. Tears flooded my face and I couldn't say anything. It was as if someone had killed my child, my own flesh and blood! Dawn got on the floor and held me tightly while she cried with me. Kenya was only twenty-three.

Chapter 6

Boss Bitch

It had been four days since Kenya's death. I hadn't been to work. I was trying to pull myself together enough to attend her funeral, which was today. I hadn't talked to Gregg, Dawn, or anyone in the outside world for that matter. I called Dawn's phone a few times and got no answer, so I knew I'd have to stop by. As I gathered my things, my mind drifted back to Gregg and that day at the hospital. I found it strange that he hadn't called since then. I remembered him being in such a rush when his pager went off. I went into the kitchen, picked up the phone and pressed redial. A woman with a pleasant voice answered.

"Lutheran Hospital, how may I direct your call?"

I hung up and pondered for a second.

"*Coincidence!*" I thought.

I didn't have time to investigate. I needed to get to Dawn's.

When I arrived, I spotted her car and bike so I knew she was home. I banged on the front door for about ten minutes before I walked around and started tapping on the window. I got no answer so I went to my car and leaned on the horn. On my way back to her door, it crept open slowly. Dawn rubbed her eyes smearing her mascara across her face.

"Okay, Okay! I'm coming, I'm coming."

She looked terrible, like she hadn't slept in days and had a hangover. Her hair was all over her head and her clothes were hanging off of her, covered in what appeared to be food stains. She had been using. I knew Dawn was liberal and that she popped Ecstasy pills and snorted coke for recreation, but this was different. Now she was using drugs to ease the pain.

"I called you!" I said pushing her aside and bombarding my way past her.

Her apartment reeked. She had an empty bottle of Jack Daniels on her living room table alongside a mirror she'd obviously been using to snort lines. I pushed aside the junk on her couch and sat down.

"Please, make yourself at home!" she said sarcastically.

"You look like shit!" I said trying to hit a nerve.

"Yeah, well I feel like it! Want a beer?" she said shrugging it off and heading towards the kitchen.

"It's nine in the morning!" I raised my voice so that she could hear me.

"Well you gotta live each day like it's your last right? You never know," she said sniffing her runny nose and flopping down on the couch.

"The funeral is in an hour and a half!"

She cracked open her beer. "You sure you don't want one?" she asked seeming unfazed.

"Did you hear what I just said to you?"

"I'm not going!"

"So let me get this straight. You're telling me you're not going to go and pay your respects to a woman who had your back through everything? A woman who risked her life for you on more than one occasion. You selfish ass bitch!" I snapped.

I grabbed a bottle of Hennessey from the table and threw it past her head at the wall. It shattered into pieces and what was left of its contents ran down the wall.

"I was going to drink that," she said unaffected.

"I told Charlotte you were getting out of control!"

"Fuck you Clarke! Don't act like you're suddenly concerned about what the fuck I do!"

"What?"

"You and Charlotte never gave a damn about me! I was always the pawn, sending me on jobs you could never handle!"

"What are you talking about?"

"Don't act dumb. You two have always been in cahoots. She called you. She called you for help and you didn't even listen. You were too busy fucking up a job or should I say *fucking on the job!*"

"I drove by her house! You know the rules!"

"Fuck the rules!" She put her hands on her head and pulled on her hair. "Kenya didn't deserve to die! That should have been me!"

I started to have regrets about coming over.

"Kenya was a good kid. She just got dealt a fucked up hand. I should've died! I should've died!" she screamed banging on her expensive stain glass table.

I thought the drugs had taken over and she didn't mean anything she was saying.

"No, we can't control fate!" I said unaware that Kenya had fired the last bullet that took her life just seconds before help arrived. I tried to console her, but she pushed me away.

"Yes, I should have, because of what I did!" she started to cry.

"What do you mean? What did you do Dawn?"

I pulled back to look at her and she began to cry harder. In all the time, we'd been killing men, Dawn had never revealed to any of us why she did it. We all had our own emotional reasons and thought pleasure was her only motive. She wiped the tears from her eyes and glared off into space.

"I've killed ninety six men Clarke!"

There was a moment of silence. I was shocked because to my knowledge Charlotte had only assigned her about fifteen.

"I don't understand."

"They just don't know it yet!" she answered.

I rubbed her hair and gave her time to regroup, but I really wanted her to just spit it out.

"His name was Trent. He was my fiancé. I came home and..." she paused. "I came home and found him in bed with another man. In my bed!" she shrieked pointing to herself. "Wearing my damn robe and night gown!"

I just listened to her.

"He was my everything, my first kiss. He took my virginity, everything!"

"What did you do?" I asked in a low voice.

"I left him, but a week later I found out I was pregnant. I went to the hospital and they told me..." she paused again and a blank expression engulfed her face.

"They told you what Dawn?"

"They told me I was HIV positive."

All of my senses went numb. I had so many unanswered questions I wanted to ask her like; how many men had she knowingly infected and was it full blown? Somehow, it all seemed to add up. The way Dawn carried herself was far from respectful her drug abuse and not to mention her job or her lack of understanding for the importance of protected sex. She truly lived each day like it could potentially be her last.

"That bastard ruined my life and forced me to take the life of my child."

"Abortion?" I asked sympathetically.

"Any man that would cheat on his woman with a fucking tranny deserves to die and a bullet to the head ain't the only way to go about it!" she said regaining her rage as she drank the rest of her beer.

I began to think of all the men I knew she'd slept with and quickly lost my mental count.

"I'm going to be late. I should go," I said not knowing if I should feel remorseful for her, the men who were walking time bombs, or their innocent unsuspecting wives. I closed the door and walked to my car in a daze.

Kenya's funeral was quaint and small. She didn't have many friends or family. I sat in the last row. Dawn and Charlotte were both no shows. That was probably for the best though. Dawn and Kenya were like sisters. I don't think she could have handled it. Kenya's mother didn't show either.

She looked so peaceful. They had done a good job hiding the bruises on her face. Tawnya seemed to be the only one overwhelmed with emotion. Her family had to pry her from the casket. I wanted to reach out to her and embrace her. I wanted to let her know that I was feeling the same pain she was if not more, but we'd never met so that just wasn't possible. As they escorted her out, our eyes met for a brief moment. She looked at me as though she was trying to place my face, like she'd seen me before, but couldn't remember where.

I couldn't watch them put her body in the ground so when everybody finished viewing her and loaded into their cars I went up to talk to her.

"Hey baby girl. You would not be happy about this dress they got you in," I smiled trying to hold back the tears.

They'd taken out her French braids and curled her long pretty hair. A single tear rolled down my face.

"I'm sorry baby girl. I'm sorry."

When I left the funeral service, I started the long drive to Charlotte's house. She wasn't expecting me, but she was going to hear what I had to say. During the hour and a half long drive, I had more time to put things into perspective. I cried out in anguish over both Dawn and Kenya. I was even more pissed that Charlotte didn't even bother to send her condolences. We were supposed to be girls. Hell, we were supposed to be sisters. What the fuck was happening to us? An establishment that took us years to perfect was falling apart in a matter of months. Without Kenya and with Dawn actively dying, what did we have left? More importantly without loyalty, there was no Charlotte Girlz.

By the time I pulled up to Charlotte's home, I was heated as hell. I rang the doorbell twice and then once long. I knew it would take her a while to answer since she wasn't expecting me. I exhaled as the video cameras zoomed in and checking the perimeter of the house.

"Yes?" her voice called out of the box.

"We need to talk."

"You alone?"

"What do you think?" I answered perturbed.

She buzzed me in and I jogged up the stairs to her office. As usual, her chair was facing the window, her back towards me.

"Cut the bullshit Loe!"

Loe was a nickname I'd given her when we were just kids. I hadn't used it in years and knew she would find it highly disrespectful, but I really didn't give a damn. She spun around in her chair.

"This is way out of protocol!" she said seriously her hands crossed on her lap.

"One of our best friends is dead. Fuck protocol Charlotte!"

"I know you're upset Clarke, but let's not lose our professionalism. When people panic they get caught!"

She poured a drink and tried to hand it to me, but I refused it.

"Professionalism?" I said exasperated.

Before I could continue, she cut me off.

"Now, obviously Kenya can't finish her job, so you'll need to reassign that to Dawn and what seems to be the delay with yours?" she asked nonchalantly taking a sip from the glass, but maintaining eye contact as she sat back down.

"Are you fucking serious?"

"*Are you?*" she raised an eyebrow. "You storm up her unannounced. You violated the code by holding a conversation over the phone with Kenya, and then you fail to finish your job!" she said reaching for a cigar.

Before I knew what had hit me I'd pulled my gun and aimed it right between her brows.

"So exactly how much money do you take off the top? You're out here living like a boss bitch while we're doing your dirty work. So what am I a henchman now? I started this shit Loe! Did you forget that? Do you have a fucking heart? Kenya is dead!" I yelled my hand beginning to tremble.

"Oh I have plenty of heart!" she said as she stood up. "And I had plenty of heart when I helped you drag that body into Lake Erie didn't I?" she contested walking towards me slowly.

I followed her movement with my gun. Even though she'd been sitting behind a desk for the last couple years I knew, she could be just as ruthless as me if not more. She walked right up to the barrel of the gun.

"Now I understand you're upset, but this is past disrespectful. Put it away!" she said slapping my hand to the side as if it weren't even loaded.

She sat on her desk and took a few puffs of her cigar. She was right. I owed her. I was letting my emotions get the best of me. In this game there are bound to be casualties. I turned and walked towards the door.

"Finish the job Clarke!" she said sternly.

I nodded my head and left.

Chapter 7

Marcia

Gregg and I had been dating for almost seven months now. With all the drama that was going on, I wanted nothing more than to be in his arms, so I called and asked to see him. He had been good to me and I planned to return the favor. A lot of women fail to realize that even early in a relationship you have keep the sex interesting. You have to fuck him so good that he won't have the energy to even *look* at another woman.

In the mirror, I admired my natural beauty, no makeup, no fillers. I ran my fingers over a scar on my left shoulder. Clyde had given it to me with a broken bottle. It healed into a flat slither a few shades lighter than my brown skin. As I oiled my body, I watched my reflection in the mirror. I slipped into my thigh high stockings, pushup bra, and garter belt. Dawn wasn't the only one who could put the moves on a man. I strapped on my black stilettos and wrapped my trench coat around my waste.

By the time I arrived at Gregg's house I was already aroused. The combination of my V-12 engine and the anticipation made my panties moist. I tapped on the door slightly buzzed from the three shots of Patron I'd drank before I left home. Gregg answered the door and before he could speak, I placed my index finger over his full lips to hush him. I backed him out of the doorway into the house and closed the door behind me. Slowly I took my finger off his lips.

"You look..."

I dropped my coat to the floor leaving him speechless. His eyes moved up and down my body, and then back up again in pure astonishment. I threw my hair over my right shoulder and started to kiss him more passionately than I'd ever kissed a man before. Our tongues wrestled back and forth, both trying to obtain the dominant position. I sucked on his bottom lip and bit it gently. I ripped off his clothes and pushed him onto the couch, taking charge. Then I walked over to his entertainment system giving him a clear view of my goodies. I popped in "*The Chocolate Factory*", one of the sexiest albums ever made. I danced in front of him while I made his hands caress my curves. I mounted him and felt my pussy become more wet when his dick pressed against my thin lace panties. I kissed his neck and licked the inside of his ear. Most men love that. I slid down to my knees, sized him up, and tried to swallow the whole thing. The skin of his dick was smooth like a Hershey's kiss. I looked into his eyes while I spit and slurped all over his big dick. I climbed back on top of him, grabbed the head, and slowly slid it into me. I gasped and so did he because it was a perfect fit. He knew this was his pussy and that no one else had been in it. I started to grind him slowly as I watched his eyes roll into the back of his head. I loved being in charge. When I knew I had him right where I wanted him, I twisted around without taking it out and started to ride him like a stallion. He groaned louder. Men like it when you talk to them dirty during sex. The dirtier the better, so I went for it.

"Give me that dick baby. I want that nut!"

He moaned louder. I got caught up in the moment and found myself bouncing on his dick even harder. "Shit! Fuck!" he yelled, his hands clenched around my small waste.

Before I could allow him to pull out, I felt his warm semen oozing inside of me.

"Where's your shower?"

"Huh?" he said still in a daze.

"Shower, where is it?" I asked anxiously.

"Oh, second door on the left."

I quickly turned on the water as hot as I could stand it and started to wash myself vigorously, forgetting that taking a bath or a shower is the worst thing you can do after a slip up during unprotected sex.

"*I put it on him,*" I thought to myself smiling on the inside.

I rinsed off, letting the water fall down my face and through my hair as I consumed the steam. As I was feeling for the faucet, the shower curtain opened and Gregg nestled his body behind mine. He grabbed me forcefully by my wrists and pressed me up against the wet shower wall. As he kissed my neck, I felt his dick throbbing against my ass. He gently kissed the scar on my shoulder. His lips made a clicking noise when they released me. Then he slid into me and started to pound my pussy. He was so deep I could feel him in my stomach. I pressed the side of my face against the wall. Water dripped down our bodies adding to our moisture. I bit my lip trying desperately not to give in, as he showed no mercy. I screamed out, exploding all over him and buckling at the knees. He turned me around and kissed my lips. He smiled, but I couldn't speak. He washed my body, even my feet. I grabbed my towel and headed towards the bedroom while he continued to shower.

"*That man is a keeper!*" I thought to myself.

As I was drying myself off his cell phone rang. "Gregg!" The water was probably too loud because he didn't answer. I laid down on the bed.

Just as I was getting comfy, the phone stopped ringing. My eyes wandered around the room and stopped at the clock. It was 1:57 AM. My first mind wondered who the hell was calling him this late, but I trusted Gregg. He never gave me any reason not to. Hell, I knew a lot more about him then I pretended to. If he ever tried to deceive me, catching him in a lie wouldn't be very difficult.

"*Then again, who the hell is calling him at two o' clock in the morning?*" I thought. I got up, walked over to the phone, and picked it up. Before I looked at the caller ID, I tried to convince myself to put it down. When you go looking for trouble, you find it. I put the phone back on the dresser and it started to ring again. I opened it. It was a 2-1-6 area code, but there was no name. I looked towards the bathroom and then back at the phone. I answered it.

"Hello?"

"Who the fuck is this?" It was a woman. "And what the fuck are you doing answering Gregg's phone?"

I've never been the type to rant and rave over the phone with a bitch, so I hit her where I knew it would hurt. "He's in the shower right now. Would you like to leave a message?" I said in a *fuck you* tone of voice.

"Shower?"

"Yes, shower!" I snapped back.

"Well, look you tell that no good nigga I hope he dies! As a matter of fact I hope somebody blows his damn head off!"

This bitch was really crazy! Before I could respond, Gregg entered the room.

"Here, you can tell him yourself!" I said handing him the phone.

"Who is it?" he asked me.

I just threw my hands up. Even though I knew he wasn't guilty I wanted to see how he was going to handle the situation.

"Hello?"

I could hear her hooping and hollering like a mad woman.

119

"Look Marcia, I told you to stop calling me. You need to move on like I have."

Her screaming became louder.

"I'm hanging up now," he said closing the phone.

I didn't have to say a word. Every bit of my facial expression said *get to* explaining nigga!

"I'm really sorry about that Clarke. I should have told you about Marcia."

"Marcia?" I raised my eyebrow.

"She's an ex-girlfriend. There's nothing between us anymore. She's kind of crazy. I didn't want it to run you away!"

Why is that always every man's excuse? She's crazy! Normally something like this would be a huge red flag, but I knew Gregg was telling the truth. Charlotte had already informed about the looney broad. Marcia was the one who hired us to kill Gregg.

"Let's not let her ruin our night okay," he said sincerely.

I laid my head on his chest and he kissed me on the forehead.

"Your confidence is so sexy!" he said caressing my breasts.

"Again?" I whined, my walls exhausted, but still yearning for his penetration. "We just got out the shower."

He simply smiled. When he entered me for the third time, my vagina had swollen to an even tighter fit. We made love into the early hours of the morning.

Chapter 8

That girl is poison

Clarke

Things between Gregg and I were going great. I looked up and before I knew it, three more months had flown by. We were planning to take a trip to Miami in the spring.

"Ms. Williams the doctor will see you now."

I walked into the examination room ready for a normal routine exam. I'd always worked out five days a week and knew I was in tip top shape.

"Any discomfort or pain when I push here?" she said pressing down on my abdomen. Her foreign accent had become easier for me to decipher over the years.

"No."

"How about here?"

"No."

"Well, I'm going to finish up your lab work and then I'll have the nurse give you your discharge papers."

"Okay, thanks doc," I laughed.

While waiting my cell phone rang. "Hello."

"I need to see you today. Five O' clock. Albert is expecting you."

I didn't bother to respond because I knew she'd already hung up. It was Charlotte. We weren't due to meet for another week or so and it wasn't like her to call an emergency meeting with me. I racked my brain for reasons why she may have wanted to see me.

"Ms. Williams."

"Yes." I turned around expecting to see a nurse with discharge papers, but was surprised to see Dr. Narra again.

"I thought you weren't dating?"

"I'm sorry?"

"You're pregnant Ms. Williams."

I shook my head trying to grasp hold of what she'd just said.

"You're going to be a mommy."

I'd been going to Dr. Narra for ten years and I trusted her judgment, but if this bitch thought Clarke Williams was pregnant she was out of her damn mind and seriously needed to consider another career choice. Me, pregnant? She's lucky I wasn't hurting for money or I would have taken her ass to court for malpractice due to misdiagnosis.

"Test me again."

She began to laugh. "Oh, Clarke it's ninety nine point nine percent accurate! The nurse will be in shortly," she said tapping me on the shoulder. "You should be excited. You are getting older. Now is a good time."

It was already three O' clock, so I grabbed my purse and left.

On the way to meet Albert, Charlotte's driver, I picked up a home pregnancy test.

When Charlotte buzzed me up, I felt a little queasy. I don't know if it was due to my supposed pregnancy or my nerves.

"Have a seat Clarke."

Surprisingly she was sitting on the edge of her desk, one foot resting on the floor the other displaying a Marques Milano black stiletto not available for purchase in the United States. I sat down uneasy and put my bag on the floor.

"How long have we know one another Clarke?"

"I don't know. Twenty something years."

"So would you say we've developed a trust in that twenty years? A bond?"

"Of course. Where are you going with this Charlotte?"

"I got a phone call today Clarke."

"From who?"

"From Gregg's ex-girlfriend. She said she wants her money back and that she's going to the police if we don't handle the job soon. She also said that a woman has been answering Gregg's phone." She slid around to the front of her desk and took a sip of champagne. "It's been seven months Clarke. Why haven't you taken him out?"

"I'm trying. He's a perfect fucking gentleman. I can't get him to kiss me, let alone get him in private," I lied. "I don't play phone games. You know me better than that. And Marcia is fucking crazy!"

"What I do know is that you need to finish the job." She took another sip of her champagne and then paused. "You have 48 hours," she said without any emotion.

I stood up and accidentally kicked over my bag. My pregnancy test tumbled out onto the floor. I quickly scooped it up and tossed it back inside, but I knew she'd already seen it. I started to walk towards the door.

"Clarke!"

I stopped.

"I never told you her name was Marcia."

I left.

The next afternoon I found myself sitting in Dr. Narra's office again, this time for an "emergency" appointment. I was getting an abortion and there was nothing she could do or say to persuade me differently.

The room was cold and in need of some serious décor. The paper on the examination table crinkled underneath me as I struggled to find a comfortable position. Dr. Narra entered the room. Her huge smile overcame her small petite stature. She spoke in a thick Sudanese accent.

"So good to see you, a bit sooner than I expected." She slapped on a pair of latex gloves. "Are you hoping for another girl, or a baby boy?"

I hesitated realizing that she thought I was here for an ultrasound. "I don't want to know the sex."

"Oh, you want it to be a surprise!"

"No. I want an abortion!"

Dr. Narra glared back at me. Her eyes were filled with confusion and genuine compassion. She knew of my miscarriages with Clyde. In fact, she nursed many of the wounds and broken bones he'd given me. She watched me transition from a meek pushover into a demanding, self sufficient woman!

"Clarke, as your Physician I cannot tell you what to do, but as your friend it is opinion that you at least obtain an ultrasound before making such a drastic decision. "What about the father? Have you spoken to him?"

126

Before I knew it, she was greasing me up. The jelly she used to lubricate my belly was thick and cold. There wasn't much of a sensation as she scrolled over my stomach, which was still relatively flat and completely stretch mark free. Dr. Narra squinted at the black and white screen trying to make out the sex of the still forming fetus. Her eyes lit up with excitement as though she had stumbled upon a hidden treasure.

"It's a boy! I'm pretty sure it is a boy!"

"A boy!" I shrieked.

Here I was Clarke Williams, a woman who had taken the life of so many men, carrying one inside of me! For an instant, I pictured the three of us, happy and married. I pictured him being a splitting image of Gregg. I thought of his first steps and his first girlfriend. I thought about how I'd teach him the right way to treat a woman, so that one day he too would make a very deserving woman very happy. Then the reality of Charlotte words set in and I realized that my relationship with Gregg was based on a lie. He didn't know the real me. He was in love with a lie.

I came to the conclusion that I'd have to schedule an appointment for an abortion at the free clinic. I didn't want to give Dr. Narra the opportunity to sway my decision by putting a bunch of sentimental bullshit in my head.

On the way back home, I phoned Gregg and told him I wanted to see him. He said he'd been dying to see me. Charlotte gave me instructions to finish the job and I intended to do just that.

At home, I struggled with the decision of how to kill Gregg. I loved this man and simply couldn't see myself pointing a gun at his head and pulling the trigger. I decided to use Cyanide, a poison undetectable to the human taste, but highly effective if given at the right dosage. Dawn was on standby in case I needed help moving his body once it kicked in.

My stomach was in knots when Gregg rang the doorbell.

"Hey beautiful!" he said kissing me on the cheek.

"Hey," I said hugging him for the last time...

"Smells good. What is it?" he asked.

"Lasagna."

"Works for me. I brought a bottle of wine," he said handing me a bag.

"You didn't have to."

"Yes I did," he said grabbing my hips and walking behind me, mimicking my footsteps.

"Have a seat. I'll fix our plates!"

"Why are you being so formal?" he laughed. "Can we relax for a while first?" he added.

I just wanted to get the job done, but I guess my hastiness was a bit suspicious. I humored him and sat on the couch. When we sat down there was a moment silence. He stared into my eyes.

"What is it?"

"Everything about you Clarke."

"What do you mean?" I responded still lost.

He turned to me and looked deeper into my eyes. "I believe that everything in life happens for a reason. Sometimes you think people will play a certain role in your life, but it just doesn't turn out that way."

"I don't understand Gregg."

"Listen Clarke, I know we haven't known each other very long, but I'm sure you're the one for me and I've never been so sure about anything!"

He started to reach for his pants pocket and I stopped him.

"Look Gregg there is a lot of things you don't know about me. I've been through a lot!" My hard exterior began to melt.

"I don't care Clarke! Whatever it is. Whatever happened in your past, I don't care! We'll get through it. I won't judge you!"

"I'm feeling queasy. I need to eat," I said evading the conversation.

"Alright, I'll fix the plates. You relax," he said genuinely concerned.

"No!" I said loudly. "I'll get it."

My heart was pounding while I was standing in the kitchen.

Leaning over the sink so many emotions ran through my body.

"Was he going to propose to me?" I thought. "Was I really about to kill the one man who truly loved me?"

I could barely fight back the tears as I swirled the Cyanide in his wine. I took a deep breath and walked out with the glasses.

"Hey, if you wanna do something so bad grabs our plates off the counter!" I teased.

"Looks good," he said returning and placing mine down first.

"Let's dig in," I said, taking one last look at the man who had completely changed my perspective on men; a man who had knocked down the protective walls around my heart, a man who loved me despite the obstacles I sent him through.

"To us!" I said raising my glass.

Just as Gregg was, reaching for his champagne glass that damn, pager went off again and he knocked over the wine.

"Damn it Gregg!" I said frustrated knowing that the delay would only give me more time to regret my decision. "*Could this be a sign?*" I wondered.

Charlotte's words echoed in my mind bringing me back to the reality of the situation.

"Turn that damn thing off Gregg!" I yelled.

"I'm sorry," he said sincerely removing the batteries.

"Let me get it. Where are the towels?"

"I got it!" I yelled frustrated, knowing I had to resort to plan B, which was shooting him.

I got up from the table and entered the kitchen.

"*I can't shoot him,*" I thought staring back at my reflection in the water of the sink. "*I love him,*" I whispered, but what was I suppose to do, tell him? He'd never trust me again if he didn't think I was psychotic. If I went against Charlotte, I would forever stain our bond. How could I explain that to her? I looked down at my stomach and caressed my unborn child. My mind raced, as I felt torn between the two of them. Before I could make a decision, it was made for me.

I dropped the wine glass when the sound of a single gunshot sent chills up my spine. I ran back to the dining room and found myself in utter shock and disbelief when I saw Charlotte standing in my home holding a 357 magnum revolver and Gregg face down in his lasagna. A small black jewelry box had fallen from his pocket onto the floor.

"Now that's the way you finish a job! Rule number four Clarke, you never catch feelings for a hit!" she said unmercifully.

I rocked back and forth, my arms around his breathless body.

"Please no! God no! No!" I shrieked.

The shock wouldn't allow me to respond to Charlotte's words.

"When a boss bitch has to come from behind her desk to handle some shit *you* couldn't deliver on, that's a problem."

I cried harder.

"Look at you. You're pathetic! You think he gave a damn about you? He was a fucking cop Clarke! You were so busy playing housewife that you missed the five o'clock news. Your face was all over it!" she yelled throwing a black duffle bag on the floor next to me. "I'm leaving and if you have any sense left, you would too."

I sat there still crying my hands covered in Gregg's blood as I heard the car peel off. She didn't leave me with much of a choice. There was a dead man's body slumped over on my dining room table. I grabbed the bag and darted to my car.

Chapter 9

Karma

When I arrived at a Motel Six it was almost eight. I hurried to catch the news. I took off my shoes, sat on the bed, and flipped on the TV.

"I'm Connie Chung and this is your eight o'clock news. Recently we reported on the story of a man's body found in a log cabin just outside of Hocking Hills, Ohio. Police believe that a young lady by the name of Kenya Morris may have been responsible. It has been confirmed that saliva found at the scene of the crime was a match to Morris. Unfortunately, investigators have said that Morris' body along with the body of Anthony Cole; also known as, *Tone* was found after a tragic robbery on the city's Eastside several months ago. Police also say that what appeared to be some sort of encrypted hit list was found in the possession of Ms. Morris. Over the last six months, investigators have been following the mysterious disappearance and murders of more than thirty men throughout the state of Ohio. Morris shown here with these two women, at Donna's Lighthouse was a known drug dealer and clothing storeowner in the city of Cleveland. Police have substantial evidence indicating that these two women may have also been involved. We ask that if they were watching they would turn themselves over to armed forces. If anyone has any information on the whereabouts of these women, please come forward."

I was frozen when I saw the pictures of Dawn and me on the screen, which had been taken from a surveillance camera, but were still a decent quality. I turned off the TV and threw the remote. I racked my brain for options of what to do next and then I remembered the duffle bag Charlotte had given me. I ran to get it. I emptied the contents onto the bed. There was a pair of scissors, some blonde hair dye, a change of clothes, an envelope with ten thousand dollars cash, and a one way plane ticket to Los Angeles scheduled to leave tomorrow morning.

I went into the bathroom to take one last look at my auburn tresses. As I chopped my hair off and watched the locks fall into the sink, I tried to be hopeful. I tried to look at Los Angeles as a new beginning. I convinced myself that I would leave behind all the hurt and pain and that when I boarded that plane I'd let go; let go of the guilt of Kenya's death and let go of the loss of Gregg.

I tried to relax by taking a long hot bath, but kept meditating on what Charlotte had said about Gregg. He wasn't a cop. He was a landscaper! I'd been to his house. Hell, I'd met his sister. I couldn't sleep through the night. When my alarm clock sounded at five A.M., it felt like I had just closed my eyes. As I ran water through my hair, it curled up and was just barely longer than a fade. I'd tried to cut it as even as possible until I could get to a hair stylist in L.A. I turned my head from side to side in the mirror. Blonde didn't look half bad on me.

134

I caught a taxi to Hopkins Airport and almost had a heart attack going through customs. I let out a sigh of relief when I wasn't raided by a bunch of boys in blue. Sitting at my gate in the terminal, I smiled as I watched a little boy climbing all over the seats as his mom looked slightly ashamed. He was adorable, but bad as hell. I had to hold back my tears when I heard his mother call out to him.

"Gregg, stop it! Sit down!"

The flight clerk stole my attention when she spoke.

"Now boarding flight 0522, a nonstop flight from Cleveland, Ohio to Los Angeles, California. We will now board first class."

I stood up and made my way towards the ticket booth.

"Enjoy your flight!" she said to a heavy set man standing in front of me in line.

"*I hope he's not seated next to me,*" I thought. They just don't make first class as roomy as they used to.

The clerk was a young pretty girl in her mid twenty's.

"I like your hair! It takes a brave woman to pull that look off!" she said smiling.

"Thanks. It's a new look for me. "

"Well you'll need it. Girl, I've been to Cali twice before and the men are drop dead gorgeous!" she said leaning in as though it were a secret.

"Hope not," I said dryly.

She looked slightly thrown off by my response. She ripped my ticket and returned the other half.

"Well, enjoy your flight!"

I envied her briefly. Her life seemed so simple. I wished I could go back to that age. I would have changed so much. I started to walk down to board the plane, but was stopped dead in my tracks.

"Clarke!" a voice called.

I was wondering how anyone could have recognized me with my new look. Everything in me was saying get on the plane and don't look back, but the curiosity was too much to bare. When I turned around, I frowned in confusion.

"Jazmine?" It was Gregg's sister.

"Shut up bitch!" she yelled pulling a nine millimeter from her waste.

That was also my weapon of choice. Any woman who could handle a gun like that was a tough cookie!

"Oh, hell nah!" I said tossing down my carryon bag.

136

Could shit have gotten any worse? I don't know how she found out I was involved in her brother's murder, but she was pissed. The hate in her eyes indicated she would have no hesitation pulling the trigger. She walked closer to me. My first thoughts were, "How *the hell did she get a piece like that in a place like this? She isn't really going to shoot me is she? Here? In front of all these people?*" Then again, if someone killed my flesh and blood I wouldn't care where I was when I sought out my revenge.

"You have the right to remain silent. Anything you do or say can and will be used against you in the court of law. If you cannot afford to appoint an attorney, one will be appointed for you. Do you understand what I just said to you?"

I couldn't even part my lips to speak. I had no heat on me to blast this bitch and I was in a fucking airport! If I even tried to run, there were security and cameras everywhere. She pulled a pair of hand cuffs from her waste.

"You're under arrest for the suspected murder, and conspiracy to murder of Brandon Stewart, Alexander Lewis, Andre Moore, Christopher Phillips, James Blackwell, and more importantly my partner of six years Gregg Thomas!"

Those last two words crumbled my world and took away any fight I had left in me. The last eight months of my life flashed before my eyes and it all began to make sense to me. Gregg had deceived me! His pager, the phone call, dinner, that day at the hospital it all came together. There was no Marcia. They'd fabricated the entire story to get close to me. As she hand cuffed me, she used a lot of unnecessary force.

"I don't know what he ever saw in you, to think that he really thought you were innocent!" she said disgusted.

I couldn't even so much as drop a tear. I was all cried out. As she and three other officers walked me through the airport, I was mortified by the whispers, stares, and points. She shoved me into the back of her squad car and radioed in.

"We got her. Any word on Dawn?"

I tuned in for an answer over the scratchy dispatch. There was a slight delay.

"Yeah, we got her."

I exhaled and fell back on the sticky seat.

----

6 MONTHS LATER...

Dear Diary

There are so many scorn women in this world, with both emotional and physical scars to prove it. Most of us women who are scorn seek out revenge and set out to scorn others. That's why so many of us are loveless and pissed! That's why we wind up missing out on the love of our life. All because we were too busy sugaring gas tanks and slashing tires.

The definition of Karma is simple. What goes around comes around. What you do comes back to you. Karma doesn't always come quick. That bitch is a motha fucka! She can show up thirty years from now when you're lying in a hospital bed paralyzed from the neck down and the only person you can rely on to feed and clothe you is some mad black women with a diary full a dirt on you!

I used to think that there were two kinds of people in this world. Those that fear Karma and do as much right as possible and those who do wrong occasionally, excepting the consequences they feel are well worth the thrill. Now I know there are three kinds of people in this world. People like me and Dawn, people who don't have shit else to lose, people who say fuck Karma!

With all the evidence Gregg and Jazmine had assembled, building a solid case against us wasn't hard. All three of my bank accounts had been cleaned out thanks to Charlotte, so I had to get a punk ass public defender. Our faces were plastered on every news channel in the states, so eventually Kenya's girlfriend figured out who I was. Surprisingly she didn't testify against me. I don't think it would have made much of a difference.

Dawn was sentenced to life without the chance of parole and I was given two consecutive life sentences. How can you give a person life in prison twice? I guess it was just a mind fuck. While awaiting trial I had a miscarriage, which was probably for the best.

CHARLOTTE GIRLZ

It turns out Gregg was given a job just like me, a job he couldn't follow through with. In the process of investigating the death of my husband, he fell in love with me. I think about him every now and then wondering if he meant all those things he said and what it would have been like to be married again. I don't hear from Dawn too much, we decided, not to dwell on the past. We both find it funny how that bitch Charlotte got off scotch free, but those are the rules to being one of us. You *never* snitch!

I pass a lot of the time writing in a journal, anything to keep me sane. Jail isn't as bad as people think it is, especially if you've bodied as many niggas as I have. The bitches in here respect me. You'd think I was a fucking celebrity or something. In fact, the word is some chick wrote a book about us and is actually making a lot of money off the shit. I've never read it personally, but if they decide to make a movie they're gonna have a hard time finding a women bad enough to play me!

The days in jail seem to clump together, but I always know Sundays. Sundays mean my favorite show on the Oxygen channel called *"Snapped."* I like watching it, but most of the women on it are just plain crazy. They didn't kill for money. Just stupid ass reasons like, to be with their lovers. I was laughing hysterically when the guard called me.

"Williams, you got a visitor!"

"Visitor?" I thought. No one had written or called me since I'd been locked up. When I finally made it to the visitation room, I saw a

140

young girl. She had to be about seventeen or eighteen. She had a baby with her. I sat down.

"You don't even know who the fuck I am do you?" she said rolling her eyes.

I looked at her harder. Something about her was so familiar, but I couldn't place her face.

"Danita? Your daughter!"

"Oh my God!" I exclaimed. "You're so big now!" I said reaching across the table to touch my child I hadn't seen since she was ten.

"Don't touch me!" she snapped. "I just wanted my son to get a chance to see at least one of his grandparents!" She began to cry. "Why? Why did you kill daddy?" she said shaking her head.

"Danita he was hurting you!'

"No! You hurt me! You took both of my parents from me and you never even bothered to call!" she raised her voice catching the attention of a guard.

I tried to calm her down by speaking in a low voice."Danita I love you."

"Love? On the news, they said you got paid to kill all those men. Did somebody pay you to kill daddy?"

"What?"

"I need answers!"

"No, I told you he was hurting you! I had no choice."

"Choice? You wanna talk about choices? What fucking choices did you leave me with huh? You weren't there to see my child born! My father will never walk me down the aisle. You left me with no choice! I don't even know why I came here," she said storming off with my only grandchild.

The rest of the day was solemn. I couldn't get Danita off my mind. I thought of Clyde and how none of this would have ever happened if I hadn't killed him. I think I came up with a million different outcomes. *What if I'd just called the police? Or filed for divorce?* I gave myself a headache and drifted off to sleep.

"Williams, you got a visitor."

The guard woke me from a much needed nap in my cell. I prayed that Danita had come back and wanted to talk things out or maybe even start fresh, but when I entered the visitor's room, I was puzzled to see another girl. She was dressed pretty provocatively for a jail visit. Her makeup was overdone and the blue eye shadow she was wearing was absolutely tasteless. It was evident that her brown eyes were contacts. Her skirt was so short you could almost see right under it and it was obvious that she wasn't wearing a bra. I stood over her.

"Who are you?"

"*Lorena Lopez*," she said with a smirk.

This intrigued me because Lorena Lopez was the code name me and the girls used for making dinner reservations. I studied her with my eyes.

"Who are you?" I asked again.

She looked around and then leaned into the table."I'm Ebony. I'm sure Dawn mentioned me," she said confidently.

"Doesn't ring a bell," I said being skeptical, yet completely honest.

"We used to dance together at the club."

I clapped my hands together laughing. "You're the chick who drugged that guy in the club and made off with his money!"

She just smiled. Before I could ask her why she was here, all hell broke loose.

"Code red, code red!" I heard the security guards calling as they locked us in the visitor's room and ran off to do who knows what.

When the coast was clear, she reached across the table and slid me a letter.

"What's this?" I asked.

"Just read it. It will explain everything!"

"And why the fuck should I trust you?" I said getting testy.

"Well, they can't give you anymore jail time, now can they?" she said dishing out a low blow.

The guards returned and said everyone was going on lockdown. I didn't bother to tell Ebony goodbye.

Dawn

Dawn sat in her cell. Six months in the slammer had made her once confident and flamboyant personality fade. She was depressed and pissed. She hadn't heard from Charlotte and though she and I were in the same facility it was a large one and the HIV inmates were kept separate. The Ohio Reformatory for Women in Marysville, Ohio was a maximum security penitentiary with several wards.

"Dinner!" a guard called clanking his keys against the metal doors.

Dawn emerged from her cell with her head hanging as low as her self-esteem. The guard escorted her to the mess hall.

"Throw that bitch's key away!" a voice called out angrily.

"You want to go back to the hole Nicole?" he responded sternly.

The hole was a small room they locked you in for punishment. It had no windows, no bed, and no heat. You'd be lucky if they fed you. Inmates had been known to go crazy after a few days spent there.

Nicole was a *"nothing better to do ass women"* who had been giving Dawn a hard time since her arrival. She had life with no chance of parole. They'd gotten into about three fights in the last six months. Nicole would taunt Dawn by throwing things at her in the mess hall, stealing her toilet paper, anything she could do to get under her skin. Dawn had no idea why Nicole didn't like her. Usually Dawn would retaliate, but she simply didn't have the energy and frankly, she was just tired of fighting.

"Aw, cat got your tongue!" Nicole teased as she mopped the floor.

Nicole's behavior had been pardoned so many times by warden. Not much of the staff favored Dawn or me so we didn't exactly receive equal treatment. In fact, in a week we were being shipped to The Metro State Prison for Women in Atlanta, a facility known for its harsh practices and high rate of inmate brutalities as well as fatalities. They'd given the prison the nickname *"Lovers Lane"* because of the high percentage of inmate relationships.

Just as the guard was closing the door, the alarm sounded.

"Code red, code red. Officer being assaulted!"

Immediately he rushed to help. They always move quick when it's one of their own. Dawn was the only inmate unlocked on her floor so he left her.

"Don't move Dawn!" he shouted out halfway down the hallway.

She leaned over the banister to try to get a glimpse of what was going on. When she turned around Nicole was charging towards her. All she could think was "*Not again*," but instead of attacking her, Nicole handed her a piece of paper and quickly resumed mopping.

"Let's go Dawn, I gotta put you back in your cell everyone's going on lockdown. I'll bring your tray."

The guard put Dawn in her cell, locked the heavy dead bolt, and then twisted his key in an additional lock. Checking to make sure the coast was clear Dawn opened the paper. It was a typed letter...

Dawn,

I know you're upset with me for not contacting you sooner, but I needed to keep my distance to ensure that I didn't draw attention to myself. Much of this is my fault; therefore, it is my obligation to make it right. In precisely one week, you will be free. The driver of the truck transferring you and Clarke to *Lover's Lane* will play his part to assist. I know we usually only operate with women, but he's official. I've also enlisted the help of two guards who plan to help out. Let's just say I offered them more than they could ever make working for the government. I will be in contact with you. I've already made living and financial arrangements for the both of you. Loyalty is one of the most important factors in being one of Charlotte Girlz. You never disrespected that and now I am returning the favor. Dawn, you are my sister and I love you. I will see you soon.

146

P.S. It is very imperative that you continue to appear enemies with Nicole. We cannot run the risk of anyone finding this letter, so please ingest it. It may not be as good as the meals in there, but it's a little taste of what's to come. Rule number one Dawn, *Loyalty*!

The letter wasn't signed, but it didn't have to be. She couldn't believe Charlotte hadn't betrayed her. She began to tear pieces of the letter off and chew them. The dry texture made it hard to swallow, but she managed.

The guard returned. "I got your tray. Its meatloaf."

"I'm not hungry," she said smiling on the inside.

"Alright suit yourself," he responded quickly closing the door behind him. "*What you eat won't make me shit*!" he said then winked as he locked the door.

She leaned her head back on the concrete wall full of hope.

"Loyalty," she whispered. "Loyalty!"

CHARLOTTE'S GIRLZ

AN INDEPENDENT FILM COMING SOON!!!

Sweet Revenge

A fragrance by Andrea "DJ Honey" Craig and Carma DeLane

Gud Karma

A Carma DeLane Foundation

About Carma:

Carma DeLane has given new meaning to the term "multi-dimensional". The Cleveland native may have a few titles under her belt, but her first love is music! Just in her early twenties she's worked as an Entertainment journalist, received airplay on a national radio station, published her first novel "Charlotte Girlz", and recently became a philanthropist as the founder of The Gud Karma Foundation.

As a child Carma found refuge from her troubled home in music .At the age of 13, the quiet and camera shy aspiring artist shared her talents with her fellow classmates. It was evident that she had won their approval when she was voted most talented of her class; truly a Cinderella story.

Soon after she relocated to Atlanta, Georgia to pursue a music career without the approval of her family and with only six dollars in her pocket. Since then Carma has released several mix tapes and has had the opportunity to collaborate with major industry artists.

Carma's message may put you in the mind of an earlier Queen Latifah, but she's always sure to find a healthy balance between; lyrical, femininity, and sophistication. Her heart wrenching anthems like; "Legacy" and "Growing Pains" speak on her hardships, creating intimate relationships with her listeners and relating to girls around the world. She is currently working on her first album. Be sure to support her hit single "Tinted Windows" by requesting it on your local radio stations!

You can contact Carma!

Visit

www.CarmaDeLane.com

for music, pics, videos and more!

Special thanks to House of Ego Photography

Models Anastasia Garcia and Stephan Midget

Models Anastasia Garcia and Stephan Midget

Music Making a Difference
GudKarma.org
A Carma DeLane Foundation

WHAT IS IT?

THE GUD KARMA FOUNDATION inspires students! We visit Ohio schools and present a LIVE concert promoting Self-esteem, ANTI-bullying, Peer acceptance, Non- Violence, and the importance of Education. We donate things like; team uniforms, prom discounts, pizza parties, and much more! This exciting and unique way of motivational speaking relates to children and young adults, leaving a lasting impression!

WHO BENEFITS?

Here's how it works... Local businesses donate products and services to Gud Karma. Gud Karma donates their talent and time to deliver those products and services to students in return for good deeds. Those students perform good deeds to improve their community, and the community supports the local businesses, creating a never ending circle of "Good Karma"!

HOW CAN YOUR SCHOOL GET INVOLVED?

It's easy! Do something positive for your neighborhood like; feeding the homeless, planting trees, or volunteering at a local church. Be creative! In return for your efforts Gud Karma will visit your school.

HOW CAN YOUR SCHOOL GET INVOLVED? It's easy! Do something positive for your community like; feeding the homeless, planting trees, or volunteering at a local church. Be creative! In return for your efforts Gud Karma will visit your school.

HOW CAN YOUR SCHOOL GET INVOLVED? It's easy! Do something positive for your community like; feeding the homeless, planting trees, or volunteering at a local church. Be creative! In return for your efforts Gud Karma will visit your school.

WWW.GUDKARMA.ORG

Visit

Girlsinc.org

Inspiring all girls to be strong, smart, and bold

Heart disease is the number-one killer of women.

Know your blood pressure and cholesterol levels.

Abuse is never O K!

If you or someone you know is a victim of abuse call

1-800-799-SAFE

and get help *today!*

An estimated 15.5 million women are living with Aids. *HIV* is the third leading cause of death for African-American women ages 25 to 44. Get tested to know your status, use protection!

Call **1-800-235-2331** for questions and testing information.

Please don't pass this book. Support the fight for the cure of breast cancer by purchasing your own copy.

A portion of the proceeds will be donated to the Susan G Komen Breast Cancer Foundation.

For additional copies of Charlotte Girlz

visit

intelligentpublishing.org

LuLu.com, or Amazon.com

Made in the USA
Charleston, SC
18 August 2012